Rerouting to Retirement

FINANCIAL NAVIGATION TIPS FROM
THE KELLY CAPITAL PARTNERS ROAD MAP

By Janie Kelly, RICP®

Kelly Capital Partners
SOUTHFIELD, MICHIGAN

Janie Kelly/Rerouting to Retirement—1st edition
29100 Northwestern Highway
Suite 320
Southfield, MI 48034
http://kellycapitalpartners.com
ISBN 9781729428078

Table of Contents

.

*To my wonderful husband, Pat, without whom I never would
have had this opportunity, and to our four wonderful boys,
Patrick, Charlie, Sean and Jack, who inspire and motivate me
every single day!*

Intro

*"Excellence requires us to never feel satisfied
with where we are."*
~Kelly Pierce

I feel so blessed to have gotten into this business of retirement planning. I have the joy of being in a career where my firm gets to help people every single day with life-changing decisions, decisions that truly have an impact on their lives. Not everyone has a career where they get to spend their day in an environment that is truly fulfilling.

Recently, my husband, Pat, who works for a Fortune 500 company, said to me, "Your day-to-day work experience is so rewarding, being able to spend your days meeting with people, helping guide them with such important life decisions." He is right. I feel good at the end of the day, knowing our firm has helped people and their families find appropriate solutions for them and their lifestyles. I witness the impact that has on these families as we meet over their lifetimes. I feel incredibly fortunate to be able to do what I love in a field with skills that are naturally in my wheelhouse. I am naturally inquisitive, so asking questions and really listening to the answers is a no-brainer for me. I am a solutions-oriented person, so I often find myself needing to dive deep for the answers.

Unfortunately, part of what motivates me is that I feel personal attention is really lacking in the financial services industry. This is part of what drives our firm to try and make a difference in this field. I hear complaints from both new clients and friends I know, saying their financial professional won't return their calls. I'm always blown away when I hear this. The financial advisor they pay has the nerve to not return phone calls to the clients? Do they realize these are the very people whose money constitutes their paycheck, even if their accounts lose money? I don't understand how advisors justify that, yet it seems to be so common.

I came into this career later in life. I was fortunate enough to be able to stay home and raise our four boys, an experience for which I will be forever grateful. This was, for me, invaluable and undoubtedly the most enjoyable time of my life. I am not sure I recognized it at the time, of course, amongst all the chaos of four boys, especially when they were babies—we welcomed all four in six years. Back then, my goals were a bit different. For instance, one of my big goals was to not have three boys in diapers at one time. My goals today are a bit more sophisticated and less physically challenging or messy. After our third child, Sean, was born in January of 1993, I kept thinking, "How can we have three boys when our oldest, Patrick, is still only 2?" When we had our 4th son Jack in 1996, we had the benefit of a few years in between No. 3 and No. 4 to catch our breath.

My later-in-life arrival on the financial services scene, in addition to allowing me to raise my kids, also gave me better insight into the fact that the needs and concerns of our individual families should always come first, period. Folks come to Kelly Capital Partners seeking our guidance and expertise. They have trusted us with the assets they have worked their whole entire life for, their life savings. We are honored they have entrusted us with this responsibility. It is very important to us that the client is comfortable with the plan we put in place, and we simply start by asking "What are your concerns? What keeps you up at night?"

The Makings of a Strategy

Financial Knowledge

A big part of what we do at Kelly Capital Partners—and something that is key for those nearing retirement—is developing financial knowledge. We love that educational aspect of our work. We find it truly rewarding to be able to share our knowledge with such an engaging audience, and we know we can make it less challenging for our audience, pre-retirees and retirees, to understand. The people who come to meet with us are truly engaged in our discussions because they really need to know this subject matter. This arguably is the single most important subject for them to focus on, for the stage of life they are in. They are always so appreciative for the new information that we share with them, and it is so satisfying to be able to help and inform people.

And who doesn't need information when it comes to retirement? One simple exercise to reinforce this point: ask yourself, how often do you get something just the way you want the first time you try it? Or, have you had experiences that give truth to the phrase "practice makes perfect?" That's the reason it can be so helpful to work with financial professionals who have years of practice. We hear over and over from the people who visit with us that our ability to simplify the experience and make it easy to understand helps them be more confident about their financial future. Finance can be complicated. Our goal is to make sure you don't tune out! Preparing for retirement involves some of the most important decisions you will ever make, and you need to know about what you are doing and why!

Individual Approach

There is no cookie-cutter answer when it comes to a person's individual or joint retirement plan. It's important to us as financial professionals to take the time to get personal and explore the logistics of each person's situation, and the ins and outs of their needs. When someone is "going it alone" for retirement, often they are hearing information that is meant for a "typical," "average" or "normal" retiree at 65 years old. Who is this "normal" person? We spend a lot of time listening to people near retirement, and we have yet to find someone we could call the "average" retiree. We all have different needs, goals and dreams. Plus, those goals change over time—remember, my biggest goals used to be diaper-oriented! So, something that might be important one year may not be the next year.

A good financial professional will understand the importance of listening to you, your story and your dreams. Only through dedicated listening will they be able to understand where you've been, and where you want to go; those are the foundations of your retirement income plans.

Trusted Financial Guidance

Trust is such a huge factor, people need to have a financial professional they can trust and rely on. People don't come through the door trusting us automatically, so we need to earn their trust and we understand that. We take our time making folks feel comfortable with us through multiple meetings so they can get to know us. This is an educational process for most people, so we go slow and take our time. Trust is a MUST! You have to trust your retirement professional.

New Struggles

Planning for retirement can be overwhelming and probably a little bit scary for some people. The sooner you plan, the more likely you will be able to retire the way that you want. To say there are a lot of things to consider when planning for your financial future is an understatement. It is important to have a plan to follow in your future. Where you end up in retirement depends a lot on the route you took to get there.

What Used to Work May Not

There was a time when most Americans had similar financial situations. They had a steady pension from their employer combined with a stable Social Security benefit and often some personal saving; this helped most Americans reach a place of leisure after their working years. Today, that road is becoming less and less accessible to people as fewer and fewer pensions are offered to employees, especially in the private sector. To top it off, the longevity of Social Security in its current form has come under question.

It's time to have a course-correction—we need to take these cues and forge a different path. If the old way of planning for retirement isn't working, are you ready to take the next step on the path toward this new retirement reality?

Economic Volatility

Recent economic factors complicate the situation further. During the Great Recession of 2008, while the market was taking a toll on retirement accounts across the board, numerous Americans were forced to dip into their savings to supplement their incomes, and, if they were nearing retirement, they had limited time to get back on track with their retirement savings.

The new period of uncertainty that we seemed to enter in 2008 actually was a big part of my financial services career. People lost their financial support when the stock market crashed. People close to me lost confidence in their income and the assurance that their money would last as long as they did. That's something I'll never forget—what could retirement look like for someone if a big portion of their assets disappeared overnight?

Longevity and Health

We know people are living longer than ever before. Medical scientists have mapped the human genome. With the advances of medical technology, illnesses and diseases that were highly terminal 15 to 20 years ago have become a pill and outpatient surgery—extending lifespans another 20 years, in some cases. According to the Social Security Administration, those reaching age 65 can expect to live another 20 years, meaning their retirement income will have to stretch over a longer period than in the past.[1] The sooner you plan, the more likely you will be able to retire the way that you want. You need to be proactive and not reactive to have a successful retirement.

Confusion

The financial services industry can have separate schools of thought. There is so much misinformation, old information, and competition that it can be incredibly difficult to figure out which talking head to focus on.

Even institutions such as the American College of Finance struggle to define and create a process for retirement income planning and then to train advisors about retirement income. There is little industry consensus as

---

[1] Social Security Administration. 2017. "Calculators: Life Expectancy." https://www.ssa.gov/planners/lifeexpectancy.html. Accessed Sept. 5, 2017.

to what constitutes the field of retirement income planning. Most professionals agree, however, that proper planning needs to include a cross section of traditional options.

At Kelly Capital Partners, we are independent. That means we aren't tied to any bank, broker or insurance company, so we don't have a bias between one product or another. We will incorporate solutions from both the insurance world and investment world. When the two are combined, they can play a powerful role in mitigating the potential risks retirees may face.

With an overwhelming amount of people ill-prepared for retirement, I wanted to write this book to talk about solutions across the spectrum in the hopes that people will listen. Studies show us that very few Americans have had a personal finance class throughout their education. We have an obligation, with our skills, talent and knowledge on retirement planning, to serve the people who are lacking in these areas. People need actual retirement planners, professionals who will take a holistic approach to a retirement solution and not just take your money and put in into an account and hope for the best, because what if the best does not happen? Then what? Have measures been taken to protect against the potential risks you might face in retirement, such as inflation, market loss, longevity? Are you liquid enough? Do you know how and when you will take Social Security and what that may do to your effective tax rate? Do you know how to withdraw money in the most tax-efficient manner? Have you completed proper estate planning, and has your plan been implemented? These are a few of the many elements our team helps clients incorporate into their retirement plans. We strongly believe that If everyone knew the value of retirement planning—at an early age—then we would have less confusion and more preparedness than we see today.

Good times.

CHAPTER 1

Income Planning

My money needs to last as long as I do.

This year, close to 4 million baby boomers—those born from the mid-1940s to the mid-1960s—will retire.[2] Not everyone will proceed to retirement on their own terms.

Some boomers will exit the workforce early, having been excellent at saving, so they can retire closer to age 50 than age 60. Then there are those who love their jobs, feel good and healthy, and plan to hang on, working until age 70 or even longer. But there are people of different ages who will not have a choice. Layoffs, downsizing, health, caregiving duties, injury … any of these could result in a retirement date that was earlier than intended. Trust me, as someone who came back to work after two decades of being out of a traditional 8-to-5, the older you

---

[2] Barbara A. Friedberg. Investopedia. June 7, 2017. "Are We in a Baby Boomer Retirement Crisis."
http://www.investopedia.com/articles/personal-finance/032216/are-we-baby-boomer-retirement-crisis.asp.

get, the less likely it is that you can get back into the workforce in a new job.

No matter what your circumstances are, we all must face certain realities and plan accordingly. That's where things get tricky. When it comes to planning for income in retirement, your circumstances won't necessarily be the same as someone else's. For instance, while some people can rely on pensions for a steady paycheck in retirement, most of us can't. Your plan will also have to account for the fact that you will probably live longer than you think. When wages stop coming in, when a person exits the workforce, there will be a gap in income to be filled if he or she expects to maintain their existing lifestyle. You'll have to add your Social Security benefit and, if you are lucky enough to have one, your pension, and examine any remaining gap and decide how to fill it.

It's no secret that we are, on the whole, living longer than ever. Yet, in my practice, I often see people underestimating their life expectancy by years, even decades. One of the first steps of income planning should be facing the fact that, if you live a long life, you may be retired for the next 20 to 30 years. Over the next two or three decades, the world could change dramatically. I mean, think about what your world, business, household, etc. looked like 30 years ago. Whether it's investments, income, home or lifestyle, don't just think about the next few years. Look into the next decade and beyond to map your future, because the longer you live, the more you will spend, and inflation will only accelerate your spending needs even more.

My husband's grandmother, Grandma Grace, lived to be age 92. When our third son, Sean, was a baby, he had bright blue eyes and blond curly hair, and Grandma thought he was a girl. She would say, "Thank God you got your girl, I don't know what you would have done if you didn't end up with at least one." I would reply, "He is a boy, Grandma. His name is Sean." A few minutes would go by, the subject would change, and soon Grandma Grace would come back around with "Oh what a pretty girl she is, I don't think you could handle another boy!"

There was a time when the Grandma Graces of the world were pretty rare. Yet, living to 90 is just not that unusual anymore, and it could very well happen to you! With a longer life comes the need for more resources on which to live. It's one thing to look at a pile of assets and think, "I could make that last for 15 to 20 years," but quite another to look at that same pile of assets and consider what happens if you need to make it last for twice that time period, to 30-plus years.

The biggest indicator of income needs in retirement, though, is lifestyle. Studies show us, on average, the income you will need in retirement is about 80–90 percent of your income before retirement.[3] Keep in mind, these numbers are largely based on income from when both spouses, if you're married, were full-time workers. If you want to use this as a planning metric, you'll want to have a very clear picture of what your needs will be. You will want to be proactive, not reactive. After all, who wants

---

[3] Sudipto Banerjee. Employee Benefit Research Institute, reprinted in Retirement Insight. April 11, 2017. "Change in Household Spending After Retirement: Results from a Longitudinal Sample."
https://www.retirement-insight.com/change-household-spending-retirement-results-longitudinal-sample/.

to be decades into retirement before they realize they've miscalculated?

Before you can know if you've saved enough for retirement, you need to know what your lifestyle costs every month. That's the part of the puzzle we find first. After that, you can match your lifestyle expenses against your income. Your true income picture will emerge when you establish how much you need vs. how much income you can reasonably expect from your various sources in retirement.

So, how do you actually determine your lifestyle needs?

The B Word

It's really about the B word. Yes, we said it. The B word, for Budget!

That's not a popular exercise, but it is a very telling one. Have you, or you and your spouse or significant other, really sat down and figured out how much you spend in any given month? We don't mean the expenses for your new boat or that trip you want to take. Those are discretionary expenses. We mean, how much money do you need every month for your day-to-day basic living expenses, such as food, rent, car, entertainment, dog food … try to be honest with yourself about your spending. Even after you've totaled it up, perhaps pad it with a little extra, just in case … and then factor in inflation.

In theory, this should be an easy exercise, but establishing a budget is hated by more people than you'd think. Even in our firm, we've had people adamantly and passionately argue why they shouldn't need to know this number—but we always win that argument. It could be people have the idea—consciously or subconsciously—that, if they don't know how they spend their money, they won't ever have to make any painful adjustments to their lives. They're following an "ignorance is bliss" or "what I don't know won't hurt me" rationale, but it's actually quite *ir*rational. In this case, what you don't know about your current spending could greatly hinder your retirement lifestyle.

Many people we have met with think that, as long as they have a steady monthly cash flow, everything is fine. But, when you retire, you will turn off the employer faucet and will have to tap your own dollars for that income flow. You need to plan for that day so your proverbial well isn't dry. A budget is the key.

Even after we've built a budget for our present-day situation, we'll have to have some idea of what a *retirement* budget will look like. People will ask me, "Can't I just use the same budget I had when I was working?" We have to ask, "Why would you want to?"

If you're not commuting, will you need the same amount of gas? If you don't need special work clothes or uniforms, will you spend the same on clothing? What about meals—will you eat out more in retirement? Less? The same? Some costs decrease or go away entirely when we retire, while other costs increase. Also, you won't be contributing to your 401(k) or other retirement plan. Don't we want to base our income needs off of accurate information? The first step will be calculating your *now* expenditures, but a close second is projecting your *future* costs.

One woman, let's call her Irene, was quite doubtful about budgeting. She just didn't want to see all her money in one place, because she felt there wasn't enough of it and it made her nervous. After we sent her several friendly reminders, she signed up for Mint.com, a user-friendly budgeting site we frequently recommend.

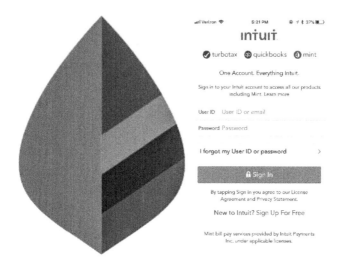

You connect your various online financial accounts so you can see where all your money is, and then you assign your different expenditures to distinct categories—you can see your bills, income and spending all in one place and set goals for yourself. She initially grumbled about having to collect so much information and enter in all her financial data, but after she started tracking her expenses and recording her budget, she had an awakening. She called me, incredulous at what she'd been spending her money on.

"Do you know, I've wasted so much money on this gym membership, and I haven't been there in months!?" she said. "And the amount I'm paying in cable is practically criminal. I'm only home enough to watch about two hours of TV a month, anyway, I can't believe I've been paying for all this stuff!"

All I could do was listen politely and nod my head. Needless to say, she credits that budgeting process with helping her find extra money to put toward other things.

You may never have lived on a strict budget in your life. During our working years, those of us who made more than we spent each month may never have even thought about it. As long as we paid off or met our debt payments, put money into investments, and paid our normal bills on time, we lived on cruise control. But now you're approaching retirement, everything you knew or thought you knew about budget and income planning is about to change.

We're not trying to scare you, we're just trying to emphasize that you shouldn't underestimate the difficulty of going from "two-paychecks-a-month" mode into "no-paychecks-a-month" mode. Having a grasp on your budget and expenses can make that adjustment smoother by helping us see the total picture, laying our outflow against our income, and letting us make better decisions by giving us better information. Ultimately, it can help us spend more confidently in retirement, and that's what we want: confidence in our future.

If you are retiring as part of a couple, it is important that both of you are on the same page—otherwise you'll be working in opposite directions. I think this is another reason people sometimes put off executing financial exercises—it can be stressful or difficult to get on the same page with your spouse. My dad used to say jokingly to his friends after a round of golf that he needed to get home to my mother, Helen, because she had probably started the arguing without him. If that's how you're thinking about this process, it may seem counterintuitive, but that makes this kind of planning even more important. Do you really want to be working at an opposite angle from your spouse when you're entering retirement?

We would argue having a strong handle on your monthly retirement budget will be the single most important factor in making sure you put your retirement money in the right places. Your paycheck is going away. Even if you plan to work part-time or only semi-retire, your paycheck and many work-related benefits will be reduced or eradicated. You'll have your monthly benefit from Social Security and perhaps you have some type of pension income, and those will pay some of the bills. But, for most of us, that amount won't be enough to live on. This means you'll need to take routine, systematic withdrawals from money you put away over the years inside things like IRAs, 401(k)s, employer plans, bank accounts, etc.

The next question becomes, do you know exactly how much you need to take from your "other" category each month to live the way you wish, for the rest of your life? To help ease the pain of putting your retirement income budget in order, we want to make it easy on you by walking you through a step-by-step procedure to help ensure you have everything included.

First, list the expenses you know you'll absolutely have in retirement, your fixed or required monthly *retirement* obligations. These are what we'll call "the basics." One way to help fill in each of these line items and track what you spend is by saving receipts. It is those little incidental purchases that go unrecorded, but many of which are necessary—last-minute household items you grabbed outside of your grocery trip, that pop-in at the hardware store to get new hinges, etc.

This is what you'd need to spend if you were forced to live in the most frugal manner, if you had literally no other money. If this happens, what is it going to cost? Let's look at the expenses that typically go in this category, starting with the largest one first.

Basics

Mortgage or rent: It would be prudent to have most if not all of your debt paid off prior to retirement, but studies show the majority of people simply don't. So, it's important to make sure if you have an outstanding mortgage or a rent payment, you have it covered.

Utilities or bills: Whether you are a homeowner or paying rent, you are going to have normal expenses, like the electric bill and the gas bill, or paying for internet or cable. Of course, some of these expenses could technically be erased if you absolutely had to, but they have become necessities for most people today.

Insurances and taxes: Don't overlook taxes, like real estate taxes or taxes you might owe on IRA withdrawals or investments. Don't forget about insurance, like health insurance premiums before age 65, or Medicare supplement policy payments after age 65. You may also have a long-term care policy or life insurance policy you pay regularly.

Groceries/food: What do you spend at the grocery store to buy food that you keep at your house? This does not include eating out; it's really just the basics. We're talking about milk, eggs, bread, etc.

Transportation: Do you have a car? Does the car have a payment? Will you always have a car payment in retirement? Have you factored in maintenance costs? How much do you typically spend on gas per month? Do you plan on traveling more or less in retirement? If you don't have a personal vehicle, have you budgeted for another transit service of some kind?

Medications: Are you currently taking any medication? Allot a monthly amount for prescriptions that you know you need to take, or even that you could eventually have to take.

Clothing and toiletries/household items: Toothpaste, shampoo, laundry detergent, etc. You also may need to continue to buy clothes, shoes, curtains for the house, a vacuum cleaner, etc.

Debt payments outside of the mortgage: Make sure you have your debt payments in your basic expense number, things like credit cards, or student loans, or a vacation home.

Health care: Many, many retirees overlook their health care costs. It's easy enough to do. After all, most of us have had health insurance through our employer. Basically, there are two paths you will go down when you retire:

One path is walked by those who retire prior to age 65 and need health care coverage until they turn 65 and become eligible for Medicare coverage.

- Have you researched what health insurance is going to cost you?
- Can you go onto your spouse's plan?
- For how long will it cover you?
- Will you be covered under the government subsidy?

You need to have a handle on what it will cost you monthly for your health insurance premiums. This will in turn affect prescription drug coverage costs as well.

The next path is walked by those 65 or older who are eligible for Medicare (which will hopefully include those who walked the first path, but after they've reached 65).

Your Medicare part B premium will be paid through your Social Security payment—which reduces your monthly benefit accordingly—but you need to make sure you have a handle on whether or not you will need to pay for any supplemental coverage. Remember, Medicare typically covers only about 80 percent of many medical expenses, leaving patients responsible in many instances for the remaining 20 percent. And 20 percent of the cost of a heart operation is a major expense for retired people on a fixed income. Hence, many people consider the need—and the expense—of having some kind of Medicare supplemental insurance.

Once you have walked through some of these things, you can start looking at the more discretionary expenses that you will want to budget for in retirement. The real "lifestyle" factors. These budget items are ones most people overlook or fail to plan for. Fun money, emergency money, ways to create joy … do you plan to travel? Spend time with the grandchildren? Then keep reading to see if you have planned for those expenses.

Discretionary

Entertainment: Are you going to spend time going to the movies, or to ball games?

Hobbies: Do you golf? Or boat? What are your hobbies and what do they cost you? How much time will you spend with your hobbies?

Dining out: How often will you go to lunch or dinner? Will you want to pay for your friends' or relatives' meals?

Traveling/vacations: Do you plan on taking trips, or traveling to visit family, or grandchildren? Are you planning to take a vacation or two each year? Will they be quick trips? Will you fly and stay in hotels, or will you drive and stay with relatives?

Home improvements: Many people put off replacing a bathroom or re-doing the kitchen until retirement. … Do you have aspirations to remodel? You should also plan to set some money aside for unexpected things, like replacing the roof or the water heater.

Family: Check out some of these other expenses. Are there relatives you'd like to plan to do these things with? Will you foot the bill for that? Do you like to buy gifts for your children and grandchildren? Do you foresee the need to financially help a child, grandchild, friend or other family member?

You also need to think about how you will spend your time in retirement.

What will your normal day, or week, look like?

If you think about it, you had a normal routine throughout your working career, and you likely will have one when you enter retirement.

How will you spend your days? Many retirees tend to have a structured week, even when retired, and having some structure or routine will help you avoid overestimating your income needs, or, worse yet, spending way too much on a regular basis.

Get a written plan that helps you meet your budget needs!

The key for success is to create this legitimate, accurate reflection of your expenses in retirement. It's a great starting point. Remember, you can constantly revisit it and adjust it whenever you want. The value of a reliable expense budget is it allows you to determine how much money you need to "make your world go 'round." This is the amount you need to bring in from your retirement savings.

You will want to revisit your budget yearly, and monitor that discretionary money to keep it from creeping in and absorbing your necessary money, which you need to cover your fixed expenses. This is particularly important as you approach retirement.

At the retirement stage of life, many things are likely changing. The household budget has been eased, as your kids are likely young adults now and no longer need support from you. You won't be contributing to your employer-sponsored retirement plans. Your tax burden may be smaller, since you won't have a paycheck coming in any more. Maybe your mortgage is paid off or you are able to downsize since you don't need a large family home any longer.

If you have a decent grasp of your annual expenses, you'll also want to consider how many years' worth you will need. We don't know how long we're going to live, but we do know we are living longer. Remember, diseases that regularly killed people even decades ago are no longer necessarily a death sentence. We can't plan on dying on time, so we have to protect against the other side of things, which might mean planning in case we live until age 105. Oftentimes I feel people underestimate how long they are personally going to live and they don't have a good understanding of the concept of life expectancy. We have people say to us, "Why are you pushing my retirement plan out so far? You know, I'm not going to live that long." But we just don't know how long we will live. The longer a person lives, the further they push out their life expectancy. For instance, an "average" male of any age has a life expectancy of age 78. But a man who has reached age 62 has just pushed his life expectancy out to age 84.[4] This is also true about making healthy choices; not only can those healthy choices translate to better living in the short term, they may allow you to live longer. This isn't a bad thing; it's about planning against the downside and making sure we

---

[4] Social Security Administration. 2017. "Calculators: Life Expectancy." https://www.ssa.gov/planners/lifeexpectancy.html. Accessed Sept. 5, 2017.

have all of the proper protections in place for the potential risks we could face in retirement.

Once you've turned each of these things into a line item, write down the sum of your expenses. Then, write down what income you'll have coming in, and from what sources. Finally, determine how much you're short, if any.

When you are comparing your expense needs with your income sources, there are a few things to consider. For one thing, which of your income sources have a guarantee of some kind? Are you using Social Security, which is guaranteed by the government, to meet certain needs? Or a pension, which is guaranteed by your company? Or are you looking to a personally funded product like an annuity, which is guaranteed by an insurance company?

Most people don't have pensions these days, especially in the private sector, so preparing for expenses with our personal savings is very important. It's never too late to start saving, and it's certainly never too early. As a parent, I'd also like to tell you that, if you have children who work in the private sector, it's never too early to get them in the savings mindset because, as much as retirement has changed for us, there is no way to tell what it might look like for their generation. I can say, however, that I don't envision many of them having pensions!

When it comes to our personal savings, comparing expense needs and income expectations is much trickier than it is with guaranteed sources. After a lifetime of focusing on accumulation, where your main goal was growing your money, your emphasis in retirement shifts to protecting your nest egg in order to sustain your lifestyle. It can be difficult for people to retool and focus on how to take this money and distribute it back to themselves for the rest of their lifetime. The question becomes, how do I take this money and make it last for my whole life? Many retirees fail to make the switch because they are still fixating on investment return instead of really focusing on turning their assets into predictable income. We think spending potential should be the focus as opposed to maximizing wealth because, at this stage of the game, you need to first make sure your income needs are met with this money and then position for growth.

Once you've measured your income needs against your income sources, you may have a monthly shortfall. This is where it's particularly helpful to have a financial professional on hand. Someone with a mind for financial strategy can help you determine how best to position your assets in retirement and which products to use to create the monthly income you need.

A financial professional can walk you through a few different methods used to create the retirement income you need:

- Method 1: Goal-based income planning (for those retirees who have a stronger stomach for risk). Strategies for this might revolve around taking on more risks for your assets in order to meet a specified rate of return that will allow you to withdraw your goal amount—such as 3 or 4 percent of your account value per year.

- Method 2: Flooring (for those retirees who have a weaker stomach for market risk). Typically, this means placing your retirement assets in products that have guarantees from governmental entities, banks or insurance companies. The goal is to meet a minimum or "floor" of guaranteed income on which you can rely for at least your basic cashflow needs, if not also your discretionary income.
- Method 3: Time-segmented (for those of you who are somewhere in the middle of the risk spectrum). Strategies here generally involve putting your money in different "buckets" of vehicles—using products with different time horizons, meaning you might draw income from one product while specifically setting aside another product from which you intend to draw income in 10 years, another for 15 years down the road, another for 20 years, etc.

No matter what method you are using to help build strategies, it's important to have a financial professional who can help keep you accountable and who can give you an objective opinion about where you are, financially.

One evening when we were speaking to a group at a financial seminar, I had a woman approach me at the end of the night. She was a nurse and she was working the shift from 7 p.m. until 7 a.m. She was 67 years old and she had a few health issues. She said to me, "You know what? I am exhausted, and I just don't know how much longer I can work. I mean, I don't think I can do this anymore."

We made an appointment for her right away and we sat down and analyzed her situation. Her house was completely paid for, because she was insistent about not taking that mortgage payment into retirement. She had been diligently contributing to her 401(k) over the years, and then actually maxed out the catch-up provision after age 50, which is when the government allows workers over 50 to contribute even more to their retirement plans in order to "catch up" on retirement savings. She ended up having a sizable 401(k). She thought she was going to have to work until she was age 73 or 74. It was a very powerful moment when she realized that was, in fact, not the case.

It's not that she didn't have enough assets to retire, she just did not know how to take all this money she had saved and turn it into income. Let me be clear, there is no "magic" financial product that could have helped her retire. But many people who come into my office, like this woman, have saved and saved, and just don't know what to do with what they have, and don't know how to put their savings to work for them in retirement.

How much is enough? How much is too much? You want to enjoy your retirement and have the money to spend on the things you want to do, you've worked for this money your whole life, you don't want to retire and sit at home. You want to be able to spend with confidence instead of worrying and stressing over every penny.

The definition of financial independence is having sufficient personal wealth to live, without having to actively work for basic necessities. Financially independent people can often generate sufficient income and/or cash flow by simply using their existing assets to meet their expenses. That income need will be different for you than it is for someone else. You have your own wants, needs and comfort level. But no matter what those are, I'm betting you are looking for financial independence and confidence in your retirement.

Vacationing in West Michigan.

CHAPTER 2

This Is Not Your Parents' Retirement

*I want to be out of money
and out of breath on the same day.*

It feels like it was only yesterday when our youngest, Jack, was 7. Some of the funniest things came out of his mouth, or maybe I just remember them better because he was our most recent 7-year-old. Our oldest niece, Lyndsey, was getting married, and her mother/my sister, Maureen, asked me if they could look at my wedding veil. Lyndsey wanted to unbox it and see if she could match it to her intended wedding dress. Of course, I was flattered and thrilled. Since we had four boys, I was resigned to the fact that my wedding things would never be out of that sealed box again.

I said, "Sure, take the whole dress if you want to, I won't be wearing it again. I don't think I can even fit into it anymore if I wanted to."

Jack chimed in, "Why mom? Did you get that much taller?"

21

Hilarious, I know. Kids really do say the darndest things.

That little boy is finishing hitting the books in college as I write this in 2018. Time is constantly passing, and with it comes change, change to which we all must adapt.

Similar to the startling amount of change that happens in our personal lives, the economic climate is one of continual change. Retirement in particular can be and has been affected by these changes. Do you remember 2008? Now, there was a dramatic economic change. In many areas, the American public witnessed the values of their homes drop dramatically. In some cases, families' homes became fiscally underwater. The ripple effect continued through the economy. People lost jobs. Those on the verge of retirement saw their personal investments dip, and many of them postponed retirement.

If you are thinking "that was an isolated event, though," consider the inflation and bubble burst on junk bonds. Or consider the after-effect of the dot-com boom in the 90s—the internet bubble burst because companies were valued much higher than their real, intrinsic values. This is actually how our economy works: A market correction is just that, a correction. In the case of the dot-com explosion, things were out of line, stocks were overvalued, and the correction brought the values back to where they should be. This should be a reminder that, when something seems too good to be true, it probably is.

Check out the following charts, covering several decades, based on the S&P 500®'s data from MarketWatch, for a refresher of what that stock market roller coaster action looks like.

S&P 500® 1960 to 1980

S&P 500® 1980 to 2000

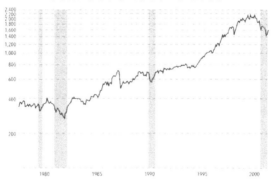

S&P® 2000 to 2010

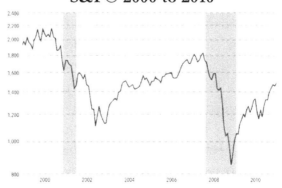

During the time following the Depression in the 1930s until about 1974, America had a retirement system that worked well. People didn't really have to worry too much about their retirement, or where their income in retirement was coming from. They were not concerned about financial markets. This is because they could fall back on retirement income from their employer, called a pension. It allowed people who were working toward retirement to have real confidence in their lives, as well as those already in retirement, benefitting from the steady income they were receiving. This was a retirement system that was simple. It did not require the assistance of a financial planner or stock broker. In fact, it was a retirement system where the employee was not responsible for any of the investment decisions.

The men and women who come into our office generally have anxiety over trying to educate themselves and know where to allocate their funds in the options they are given by their employer, to help ensure they are on the right track for growing their 401(k) efficiently and effectively. This problem did not exist before 1980, because employees benefitted from a highly educated and experienced professional pension manager making the decisions about investments in the company plan. This manager was managing money for thousands of employees ranging in age from young employees in their 20s to those in their 60s and beyond. This pension had a very long-term investment time horizon because it could have been up to 40 or more years until some of the employees would retire. The pension manager could make very long-term investments, less affected by short-term market fluctuation and economic cycles.

Then in 1980, companies wanted to remove themselves from the risk of paying the employee a pension for the next 20, 30, 40 years or even longer, so some company pension managers turned to life insurance companies. They turned to the life insurance companies as a solution, so the pension manager could turn over a lump sum of money, needed to create a guaranteed pension for as long as the employee lived. They didn't give the money to the banks, because the banks don't have the ability to provide a guaranteed income for life. They did not give the employee's pension money to Wall Street, as they do not have the ability to guarantee a pension for life. The Great Depression had left painful scars about the financial institutions in the minds of Americans who were seeking financial security. Life insurance companies are in the business of guarantees. They understand how to provide both guarantees at death, known as life insurance, and guarantees for longevity, known as annuities. The guarantees that annuities provide are backed by the financial strength of the issuing insurance company, so it's important to ensure you are working with reputable, highly rated companies.

Today, millions of retired Americans are confidently receiving what's similar to a "pension" payout via annuity income payments from insurance companies. They will get their check for the rest of their lives, if they choose. The insurance company system of retirement income can work for many.

When we compare our clients who have pensions from their employers with those who don't, we are reminded how simple their retirement decisions are. They don't have a lot of decisions to make, they know they have their pension income and Social Security benefit. Sometimes that is even enough to guarantee their lifestyle incomes, especially if they're married and both spouses receive a pension. We generally find they are able to retire earlier, have the financial freedom to enjoy their retirement lifestyle without worrying about where their income is coming from, and have less confusion. For our clients who don't have pensions, they are often concerned about a downturn and what might happen to their 401(k) if that happens. It's a constant circle of wondering, when can they retire? Or will they run out of money? The stress of having to make investment decisions for their own money can be quite daunting for the average employee, even if they are in the financial services industry.

In 1980, Congress passed legislation that implemented the 401(k). For the first time, employees had to learn how to invest for retirement on their own. The American employee now had to figure out on their own how to invest their money in the 401(k), how to take on the market risk. They had to make these decisions many times. often without any education as to how to invest money or any education on money management. The baby boomer generation became the first generation forced to transition from defined-benefit retirement plans to do-it-yourself-plans like the 401(k) and other defined-contribution plans. There are no guarantees in the investments available in most 401(k)s. There is no predetermined retirement income benefit. When you reach retirement, there is no specific dollar amount that you will receive, unlike a pension, which is guaranteed for life.

In general, people today are spending more of their income during their working years and saving less, so they have less money set aside for retirement. Plus, people are living longer than ever before. Remember, you could live 20, 30, even 40 years longer than people a couple of generations ago. Without defined-benefit plans that were the rule of previous generations, preparing for retirement (whether through a 401(k) or other means) falls squarely on each individual's shoulders. Lastly, Social Security, the retirement system in which almost everyone has a stake, in one way or another, will need government reform to continue paying full benefits beyond 2035.

There is ONLY one financial product in the marketplace that can deliver on the promise of "a guaranteed lifetime income stream." People love them or hate them; almost everyone has an opinion about them. What is it about them that so divides the affection of the American retiree?

I am talking about ... annuities!

In general terms, an annuity is an insurance contract in which you pay the insurance company a lump sum of money in exchange for their guarantee of paying you an income stream, either immediately or at some designated point in the future. An annuity is not a pension plan, nor is it part of the Social Security system.

However, pension payments are similar to annuity payments. A pension can be either a joint-life annuity (where your spouse gets your payment if you die) or a single-life annuity.

Social Security payments are also similar to annuity payments. We pay into an annuity-based trust fund all our working lives in return for the promise of payments later.

When you think of an annuity as an income-producing financial product, an annuity by itself is pretty straightforward. But, annuities can actually be more complex because they are sometimes sold or recommended for reasons other than solely producing income. Today, annuities are sometimes marketed as a vehicle for conservative growth, or for an enhanced death benefit feature, or for living benefits, or as alternatives to traditional long-term care insurance. The main reasons to buy annuities are either to provide supplemental income now or at some point in the future, and often also for conservative accumulation potential.

If you're one of the majority of Americans who say they need to receive a reliable monthly check when they retire, one way to do that is through an annuity. Annuities are not right for everyone, and, with all the misinformation out there, you should always make sure you have a thorough understanding of an annuity and how it works before you make any decisions.

Before I get into the various kinds of annuities, I'd like to cover a few "vocab" words:

Annuitize: Annuitization is when you convert the premium you've paid into your contract from a lump sum into an income stream, and, with few exceptions, it's an irrevocable decision. This typically is set up to pay the money, plus any interest, back to you over a specified period of time (five, seven, 10 years, etc.) for the remainder of your life, or even for the remainder of both your and your spouse's life. Under an immediate annuity, where payments begin immediately and there is no option to defer, the insurance company will keep the remainder of any value left in your contract upon your death. It's this piece that led to the prevalence of optional income riders on deferred annuities.

Income Rider: An income rider is an added contract feature that is available at an additional cost, typically 1-2 percent per year of your contract value, although this amount can vary widely by policy. With an income rider, you are guaranteed to receive income from your contract without ever annuitizing.

There are generally two categories of annuities: an immediate annuity and a deferred annuity. Both use YOUR money for at least a portion of the income payment, paying it out to you in regular installments.

An *immediate annuity* begins payments immediately. So, if you want your payments to begin within the first year, you might want to investigate an immediate annuity. Once income payments begin, the transaction is irreversible and you no longer have access to your assets in a lump sum. Buying older immediate annuities used to mean you would forfeit any remaining value in the annuity to the insurance company when you die, but these days there are often ways to structure an immediate annuity to ensure your beneficiaries receive the remaining value at death.

A *deferred annuity* begins payments at some time in the future. If you want to defer receiving payments until sometime in the future, when you retire, for instance, you could consider a deferred annuity. You won't pay taxes on any of the interest until you withdraw money from the annuity or you annuitize it.

There are two types of deferred annuities: variable and fixed annuities.

A *variable annuity* is a deferred annuity that provides a *variable* rate of return based on the performance of professionally managed portfolios in which your money is invested. Compared to other types of annuities, a variable annuity gives you greater growth potential. This is a bit of a "horse of a different color," because it doesn't guarantee your contract value, it only guarantees that your beneficiaries will receive a death benefit.

A *fixed annuity*, as you might have guessed, is a deferred annuity that earns a fixed rate of interest for a certain period of time. Both the interest rate and the period of time for which it will apply are determined by the insurance company.

There are two types of fixed annuities: a traditional fixed annuity and a fixed index annuity.

A *traditional fixed annuity* provides a fixed surrender charge period and a fixed interest rate guaranteed for a specific time period. You can calculate the minimum value of a fixed annuity almost to the penny if you know the interest crediting rates.

A *fixed index annuity* guarantees the value will not lose money due to market risk—just like a traditional fixed annuity—and has the potential to earn higher interest than a traditional annuity. The interest is declared by the insurance company and is based on a formula that is linked to changes in a stock market index. The interest rate is limited by the insurance company through various crediting methods.

Let's look first at some of the "bad" rap that goes with annuities.

Mostly, if you search the internet trying to find information on annuities, you are going to find a slew of articles and opinions that say you should stay away from annuities. "Don't touch an annuity with a 10-foot pole!"— "I hate annuities and you should, too!"—"Why would you ever buy an annuity, ever?"

It's important that you understand the majority of these opinions are there for a reason. And the reason isn't because an annuity is something to be avoided at all costs. A good number of negative opinions are based on a lack of understanding.

While some of this misunderstanding is about how annuities work, it is also in part because they are unfamiliar in general—while most people over age 30 have a decent understanding of what it means to have insurance or own stock, many people haven't heard a lot about annuities, period. The funny thing is, annuities are one of the oldest financial products out there. One of the earliest annuity programs was in the Roman Empire—soldiers pooled a certain portion of their pay so they could rely on income payments to themselves or their families later in life. In 1776, before the Founding Fathers even signed the Declaration of Independence, the soon-to-be-U.S. government passed the National Pension Program for Soldiers, which provided annuity payments for those who served in the Continental Army.[5]

One other reason for chronic annuity misunderstandings I think comes down to a fundamental problem in the financial services industry—there are two sides of

---

[5] Think Advisor. May 8, 2012. "Slideshow: The history of annuities." http://www.thinkadvisor.com/2012/05/08/slideshow-the-history-of-annuities?slreturn=1504623669&page_all=1.

the equation that are constantly at battle or odds with each other. On one side of the equation, you have companies who focus on insurance only. Their agents tend to think all your needs can be met with the right life insurance or annuity contract. After all, those are the only tools they have at their disposal. On the other side of the equation, you have investment companies with brokers whose strategy is to put your money in the market, stocks or mutual funds, and some might dismiss the idea of insurance contracts—perhaps because their licensing only allows them to work with market-based products. The Kelly Capital Partners team operates under the idea that it's better to offer financial planning that includes products from both the insurance and the investment world—while one person on the team might be insurance licensed, like myself, another person can bring a securities perspective to the table, like my son, Patrick. I prefer this approach, since it means our team of professionals can pull together diverse products that are more tailored to your specific situation.

This is similar to a builder's toolbox. For instance, we just added on a library to our house, and if our builder had just showed up with a hammer, I would have stopped him and asked, "Where is the rest of your tool belt?" I want a full tool belt. For us, it's not about any specific product, it's about the plan. So, whatever vehicle we need to use to accomplish our client's objective, we have available to us.

One reason annuities get a bad rap has to do with that earlier vocabulary word, annuitize. What people don't know is that there are a lot of ways to NOT annuitize today, so you can have control of your money and it will go to your beneficiaries upon your death. For some people, the risk of dying midway through an annuitized contract and having the insurance company keep the remaining contract value isn't nearly as high as the risk of running out of money due to longevity.

Some people disparage annuities because they aren't liquid. Most annuities have surrender charges if you try to withdraw your money outside of the contract's penalty-free stipulations. This is a valid point, and that is why the annuity has to be the right fit for the person's situation. An annuity certainly would not be right for all of a person's assets. Hence the reason you need a financial professional with a full tool belt.

One of the complaints I hear about annuities is that they are expensive. With certain types of annuities that is very true. But oftentimes, especially in the media, expensive annuities get lumped in with all annuities, giving a negative connotation for annuities as a whole.

The variable annuity is often viewed as one of the more expensive products you can own. According to a MarketWatch article, a variable annuity can average between 2 and 2.25 percent in annual fees. On some variable annuities, the fee can go as high as 4 percent. Also, there is a sub-account charge. Since variable annuities are investments, meaning the money is invested in securities products, they have costs associated with mutual funds or exchange-traded funds, or whatever stock market products they invest their money into.[6]

---

[6] Michael Fertig. MarketWatch. Dec. 31, 2015. "Annuities in retirement: a true guarantee?"
https://www.marketwatch.com/story/annuities-in-retirement-a-true-guarantee-2015-12-31.

Fees of fixed annuities differ from those of the variable. A basic fixed annuity or fixed index annuity contract has zero annual cost; they aren't free, by any means, but the commission that goes to the insurance agent who sells the annuity is factored into the overall costs, which are built into the product's pricing structure. The interest rate on fixed annuities reflects deductions for the insurance company's expenses and profits.

Now, both kinds of fixed and variable annuities have the option of adding riders, which usually cost between 0 to 3 percent of your contract value per year. So, expenses could add up that way.[7]

Some people automatically turn away from annuities before even learning about their benefits. Be sure to check them out for yourself because they are not for everyone.

Like all financial products, aside from the cons or bad things, there are a slew of good things about annuities, and the main thing is they can provide guaranteed, reliable, predictable income you can never outlive, bar none.

So, if you wanted to use an annuity as part of your retirement strategy here's what that could look like:

Principal protected from market risk with the opportunity for conservative growth: If you are looking to protect a portion of your long-term assets from possible market losses, an annuity could be a way to do that.

Supplemental income: If you know your Social Security and/or pension income won't be enough to sustain

_____

[7] Annuity.com. May 5, 2014. "Fees and expenses associated with variable annuities."
http://www.annuity.com/fees-and-expenses-associated-with-variable-annuities/

your basic lifestyle in retirement, some people like to use a portion of their personal savings to purchase an annuity to have guaranteed supplemental income.

At Kelly Capital Partners, we often look to annuities for direct cash flow income planning. What does that mean? Let me give you the hypothetical example of Bob and Mary.

Perhaps Bob owned his own mechanics shop and Mary was a teacher. They are 62 and want to retire at 65. They've completed the budgeting exercise from Chapter 1, and they figured they would like to have $4,000 per month to cover their current lifestyle plus their expected retirement hobbies plus health concerns. With Social Security and Mary's small state teacher's pension, they'll have a guaranteed check for about $2,500, which leaves them $1,500 per month that they will need to find an income source for.

Now, let's say Bob and Mary are fairly risk averse, that is, they don't like the idea of taking their monthly income check from a stock market account. So, instead, we'll help them figure out how much they might want to set aside for emergencies in liquid accounts like a bank savings or checking account, and then we'll help them figure out what portion of their assets they should set aside or save in a guaranteed income product like an annuity. We'll take their income goal, their time horizon (in this case, three years, because that's what their goal is for retirement), and help them figure out how much they would have to set aside to be able to not give their lifestyle needs another thought. That's what we mean by income cash flow planning.

The problem we find is not in the products themselves, but in the education of consumers. Many people come in our front door having heard buzzwords and hearsay instead of having had a solid education about what retirement—and retirement income planning—entails. From the ins and outs of annuities to what to expect in terms of savings levels and what different products can do, there is such a difference between thinking you have financial protection and knowing you do.

Like a car driver who hears a strange noise in his engine and turns up the radio instead of going to the mechanic, many people are reluctant to peek at their finances because they are scared of what they will find. Others assume their current financial professional has taken care of it all for them. Sometimes I hear "Oh, my broker says I'm invested in safe stocks." I'm not here to denigrate stocks. But there is no such thing as "safe" stocks. Stocks don't have guarantees, and they are inherently risk-based products. Your broker may have invested your money in conservative, blue chip stocks, but they still aren't "safe." That's a lack of consumer education right there.

It's funny, we'd all like some measure of protection, but not everyone knows what that means. All four of our sons played hockey in their youth. Starting in September, we'd be stuck at a rink somewhere, until April ... when spring hockey season began and went to June!

It all started in 1995 when Patrick, our oldest, was 5. There was such a demand for ice time, the rink manager would schedule the "pee wees" for 5:30 a.m. practice. To avoid the chaos of the locker room, we'd dress our little ones at home and drive to the rink in full gear, skates and all. One morning, my husband had Patrick all dressed in his hockey equipment, with pads, mouth guard and helmet, and he practically thought he was Kevlar. We got in the car, Patrick hopped in the back seat, and my husband routinely instructed everyone to buckle-up.

"Why?" Patrick asked from the back seat. "I think I'm already pretty protected!"

Yes, I do miss this chaos.

CHAPTER 3

Social Security

*Reality: Life expectancy is much longer today
than when Social Security was created.*

I can remember sitting in a political science class at
Michigan State. It was in one of those beautiful build-
ings in the original part of campus, really old with tons
of character, and I loved that class. Our professor was
very insightful and he told a lot of stories. He listened to
our ideas and encouraged us to express our opinions.
One day we got into a very lively discussion of government benefits and entitlement programs. He looked at
all the students rather seriously and said "When you all
get out into the workforce, the first thing you better do
is start saving. Save for retirement."

That was a strange concept to me, the college student,
who was most concerned about paying off my student
loans once I got a job. I remember thinking, "What? Seriously? I haven't even graduated college yet." I mean,
my professor was a smart guy, but what was he even
talking about?

He went on to say, "There is no way Social Security will be around when you are ready to retire. You are going to have to rely on your own savings."

At the time this book is being written in 2018, that was 35 years ago and I am now five years away from my earliest Social Security option, which is a reduced benefit at age 62. Thankfully, my professor was at least wrong in that Social Security is still around. It just will require a bit of reworking to meet most of its obligations.

Like most programs our government puts in place, Social Security is overly complicated. While not all strategies will apply to every person since it is dependent on a person's unique situation, there are more than 550 different ways for married couples to take Social Security benefits.[8] So you will want to do your research before you go in and fill out the paper work. I had a client, Tina, get in a two-hour line at the local Social Security Administration office, and when she finally reached the counter, she began to ask questions to the Social Security employee who greeted her. Tina wanted to know how to maximize her monthly Social Security benefit. She had questions like, "If I wait another year, but my husband takes his now, how much more will I have, or should I wait two years?" She had several different scenarios she was thinking about, and the SSA employee interrupted her to say, "Oh no, we're just here to help you file, this line is to fill out paperwork."

To be clear, since Social Security is a benefit you have earned, no one, not a financial professional, not an SSA

---

[8] Center for Retirement Research, Boston College. September 2012. "Social Security: There Is a Better Way."

employee, can tell you how to take it. But working with a financial professional who understands your goals and circumstances means you can see where your Social Security decisions will fit or how they might affect the rest of your finances, giving you the information to make the decision that best works for you.

The Social Security Administration has many informational resources, at www.ssa.gov, where they spell out the different rules in plain English, and I would encourage anyone to take a look. However, you have to manually input your information into their calculators and study the various ways the rules apply to your specific situation. Our firm has invested in software that allows us to input different scenarios to help our clients determine what each scenario looks like for them, factoring in different Social Security strategies, based on that person's specific needs. Providing this analysis is our way of filling a void that is not provided by the Social Security Administration. It is part of the retirement income picture we put together for every one of our clients.

The overall goal here is attempting to reduce the No. 1 fear most people have today as they approach retirement. That is, the fear of outliving their money. We try to reduce this concern by employing strategies designed to help your retirement nest egg last longer than you do. Foremost among those strategies is helping you figure out the Social Security piece of it.

It is essential to understand how Social Security retirement benefits fit into your overall retirement income plan. For too many people, sadly, Social Security is their only source of guaranteed retirement income. For others who have initiated retirement planning and saving, it is a piece—though often the biggest piece—of a puzzle. Even then, getting the various pieces of that puzzle to fit together can be a challenge.

The Evolution of Social Security

The Social Security Act was signed into law by President Franklin Delano Roosevelt in 1935. This Act created a social insurance type of program for people who were retiring. They had to be age 65 or older to receive this benefit. Back then, the life expectancy for an average male was age 58, and age 62 for women. The Great Depression was a catalyst for the Social Security Act of 1935. With many hardworking Americans thrown into poverty, FDR asked Congress to agree to provide a safety net for the elderly. According to the SSA, it has never been intended to be the sole source of income for retirees.

Legislation over the years has developed and reformed the program. For instance, as the cost of living increased over the years, Congress every year or every few years would legislate an increase in Social Security benefits to keep up. In 1975, Congress finally set a permanent cost of living adjustment, tied to the Consumer Price Index. When the Consumer Price Index shows that goods and services increased in a given year by a certain percent, Social Security benefits will increase in proportion to make sure retirees don't lose purchasing power. Then, in 1983, the system was overhauled to restrict withdrawal methods and adjust expectations for longer life expectancies. Yet, with increasing lifespans and declining birth rates, the country has known for a while that the proportion of people paying into the system is shrinking, while the portion of people withdrawing benefits is growing.[9]

Up until 2010, the amount of payroll dollars flowing into the system was higher than the amount of money that was needed to fund benefits. The "extra" money for the program has generally been invested in special, untraded Treasury bonds. Thanks to interest from the Treasurys and taxes on higher-earning beneficiaries, the Social Security system still takes in a bit more money than it pays out each year, but that will gradually change as our population continues to age.

There is a rough deadline of 2034 for Congress to work it out. The sooner our Congressional representatives decide what reforms to instill, the better, so changes will be more gradual and predictable for beneficiaries and taxpayers.

Timing Social Security Decisions

Social Security wasn't meant to be 100 percent of a retiree's income: The Social Security Administration estimates that, for those with "average earnings," Social Security benefits will replace 40 percent or less of a monthly retirement income.[10] And yet, many Americans

---

[9] Social Security Administration. "Historical Background and Development of Social Security."
https://www.ssa.gov/history/briefhistory3.html.
[10] Social Security. 2018. "Prepare for Your Financial Needs."
https://www.ssa.gov/planners/retire/r&m6.html.

rely on their Social Security check for the majority of their income.[11]

Social Security averages your 35 highest years of earnings and applies a formula to determine your primary insurance amount. So, it is not the longest amount of time that you worked for; it's your highest 35 years of wages. If your last five years are your highest wage-earning years, then those wages will be accounted for in the calculation, so it may make sense to keep working to help increase your Social Security payments. But if the last five years are the lowest wages you've ever earned, then that's another thing to think about because it might not make much difference in your total Social Security benefit amount if you stop working.

To understand Social Security's place in our overall picture, we first must understand a principal cornerstone of the system. That is, that the timing of when we first begin to take benefits sets a payment standard that— with the exception of annual cost-of-living adjustments—stays with us the rest of our lives.

The bottom line is a larger monthly Social Security benefit awaits those who wait until later in life to begin taking benefits. The full benefit you are due based on your earnings awaits you at full retirement age (FRA). Your FRA is basically the point that the government says people your age should consider retiring, and depends on the year of your birth. For those born in 1937 or earlier, the full retirement age is 65. For people born between 1943 and 1954, the full retirement age is currently

---

[11] Social Security. 2017. "Fact Sheet."
https://www.ssa.gov/news/press/factsheets/basicfact-alt.pdf.

age 66. For those born in 1960 or after, the full retirement age increases by two months per year until age 67. You can begin taking benefits at 62, but if you begin taking Social Security before FRA, for every year you are away from FRA, your monthly check will be a little more than 6 percent smaller than it would have been at FRA. Conversely, for every year that you wait to begin benefits after FRA—up to 70 years old—you can increase your monthly check 8 percent. They call these increases DRCs, or delayed retirement credits.[12]

At age 70, your monthly Social Security check is not going to get any larger if you wait. But consider for a moment the return you will have received in waiting until then. Those 8 percent annual DRCs until age 70. … Is there anything out there that can guarantee 8 percent annual growth?

Let's plug in some numbers to show how this might work.

Let's consider a person whose earnings will produce a monthly benefit of $2,000 at age 66, his full retirement age. That person would see his benefit reduced by 25 percent—by $500, that leaves him $1,500 a month—if he elects to begin taking Social Security benefits four years early at age 62. Conversely, this same person will see his annual benefit increased by 32 percent—thanks to growth of 8 percent a year over four years—if he waits to begin taking benefits until age 70. At that time, his monthly benefit will have grown by $640 a month, to $2,640 at age 70.

---

[12] Social Security. "Benefits Planner: Retirement." https://www.ssa.gov/planners/retire/retirechart.html.

Let's repeat one more time as a point of emphasis that the benefit you receive when you first take it is the amount you will receive for the rest of your life with small adjustments only for cost-of-living increases.

The theory behind getting a reduced benefit when first taken at an early age is simply stated: Because a person taking benefits early will, in theory, receive more payments over a longer period of time during normal life expectancy, those payments must necessarily be reduced. The person who waits to begin taking benefits will in theory receive fewer payments in a normal lifetime, so his benefit must be greater in order to even things out. Studies have estimated the total benefits paid to persons upon first taking Social Security at age 62, at age 66 or at age 70 equal out somewhere around age 79 or 80. If you live longer than that, you could be tens of thousands of dollars ahead in total benefits if you wait until your FRA or even later, to begin taking benefits. If you don't live that long, you could leave money on the table.

The problem, of course, is that none of us know how long we will live. We might have a general idea based on our current health or family history of longevity, but the overall trend in American society today is to expect a longer average lifespan. Today's seniors, on average, are living longer than any previous generation. That's good news, but it comes with challenges in the form of increased medical care and possible long-term care expenses—costs that represent the biggest drain on a typical retirement nest egg. Longevity also increases exposure to inflation, meaning your retirement savings over time may not buy as much as they once did.

Many times, people will say to us, "Why are you pushing out my life expectancy so far in my retirement plan here? You've got me living this really long life. I'm not going to live that long." What they seem to be missing is that life expectancy is a "mean" kind of average. Not mean as in spiteful, but mean as in everyone's life expectancy gets put in the same pot and divided equally. But what it really means is that half of people are going to live beyond (perhaps *well* beyond) that life expectancy. For instance, the "average" life expectancy for a male today is getting close to 77, but if you are healthy and you're 62, actuarial tables are saying you're going to live closer to 84.[13]

We don't know what is in store for us, so we should consider how we're planning for an income we can never outlive. If you delay your Social Security and you do live a long time, this could give you a larger amount of money to live off of for the rest of your life.

Considering all these factors, it seems obvious that strategies to make the most of Social Security benefit checks—typically the biggest source of retirement income for most people—have an essential place in any retirement plan. But it's not as simple as "everyone should delay benefits until 70." For some people, delaying their Social Security withdrawals is feasible. For others, there may be very good reasons to start distributions early.

When it comes to deciding when to retire, most people just want to leave the hectic workaday world, or take

---

[13] National Center for Health Statistics. 2016. "Health United States Report 2016."
https://www.cdc.gov/nchs/fastats/life-expectancy.htm.

a more limited role in it. Others may need to stop working for whatever reason; maybe they have a health issue, maybe they're going to stay home and care for a loved one, a parent or a spouse if they are ill. Maybe they have been downsized out of their job, or their job has been eliminated and they can no longer work in that position, and then they're having difficulty finding employment. Another reason people retire early can be the emotional stress of the job or the physical labor intensity that the job requires, when that person is no longer physically able.

I had a client who had driven a big rig for 30 years. The trucks and other heavy equipment Tom drove were difficult to control—they shook, they were old, his schedule was erratic, and the physical conditions were just plain hard. It was difficult on Tom's back and kidneys, and he was suffering from chronic pain. He had built a decent pension and had an inheritance, but he was scared to leave his job. He was only 57, and, despite the obvious fact that his work was wreaking havoc on him, physically, he didn't have a thorough understanding of his financial situation. It turned out he had more than enough resources to meet he and his wife's income needs, plus a substantial reserve. After she had watched him work this job for decades, his wife finally said to me, "Please, look at Tom and tell him it's okay, that he can retire and we will be okay." I was able to look him in the eye and do so. For Tom, much of the decision to retire came down to confidence in his financial situation. After he retired, Tom had a regular schedule, and happily told me he's lost a lot of the bulk that he'd maintained as a truck driver, in turn easing his chronic pain.

Like Tom, there are many, many reasons people retire early or before their full retirement age and, if that's the case, sometimes it makes sense to take Social Security earlier than your full retirement age. We'll get into this a bit further on.

It's also important to remember that, no matter their FRA, a person will become eligible for Medicare on the first day of the month he or she turns 65. Enrolling earlier or at that time is of paramount importance because, if you delay enrolling for even two months after your birth month, you may have to pay a higher premium for Medicare Part B and related coverage, PERMA-NENTLY. The reason this is relevant to Social Security is that many people lump their Social Security and Medicare benefits together in their minds. This is a mistake—one that can be costly!

Spousal Benefits

Spousal benefits for Social Security become a little bit more complicated in their strategy. If your spouse has not qualified with the 40 credits necessary to earn their own retirement benefit for Social Security, then they're considered to be a nonqualifying spouse. If they have been married at least a year, or are the parent of the qualifying spouse's child, they can collect up to 50 percent of the qualifying spouse's benefit at full retirement age. To start the spousal benefit, the qualifying spouse must have started collecting their benefits. If the qualifying spouse takes benefits before their full retirement age, then the nonqualifying spouse's benefit will be reduced accordingly. If the nonqualifying spouse takes benefits before full retirement age, this will also reduce their benefit. However, the nonqualifying spouse will never be eligible for more than 50 percent of the qualifying spouse's benefit at full retirement age—it will not increase the spousal check for either the nonqualifying spouse or the qualifying spouse to delay taking Social Security payments past full retirement.

When a spouse dies, the household will only receive one benefit, whoever's check is higher. This means, if your spouse had a higher benefit check, you, the survivor, will now step into those benefits, and your own lower benefit check will be eliminated. While it is good that your family will preserve the higher check, it is unfortunate you will then be living on one check less. Since you will still have the same cost for your home, taxes, insurance, etc., your lifestyle needs will likely not decrease by much.

If you are divorced, you might be eligible for a retirement benefit based on your ex-spouse's work record. You must have been married for at least 10 years. Divorced benefits are pretty much the same as spousal or survivor's benefits, except that you don't have to wait for your ex-spouse to file before you are eligible for a divorced spousal benefit.

These general rules can be affected if you are disabled or have children under 18, but we've laid out the rules that are most important for those approaching retirement.

Taxes

We want to touch on taxes and Social Security, because this is a question we get all the time and it's just like everything else with taxation: It's complicated. Your Social Security benefit might be taxable. If your "provisional" income is less than $25,000 if you are single or the head of household, or $32,000 for a married couple, then there's not any tax on your Social Security benefit.

To calculate your provisional income, add your adjusted gross income (what you would normally report on your taxes) plus 50 percent of your Social Security income, plus any tax-free interest you've earned on municipal bonds in the last year.

So, if your Social Security benefit amount is $20,000 per year, only $10,000 will be added to your other income sources for the year. If you are single and you make over $25,000 in your combined income, then 50 percent of your Social Security income is taxable. If you make $35,000 and more, then 85 percent is taxable. If you're married filing jointly, your Social Security benefits will be taxed at 50 percent if you have more than $32,000 in combined provisional income, or it will be taxed at 85 percent if your provisional income is over $44,000.[14]

The following table may be of use in helping you calculate your taxable Social Security (these tables are current as of 2018 but may be subject to change).

---

[14] Social Security Administration. "Benefits Planner: Income Taxes and Your Social Security Benefits." https://www.ssa.gov/planners/taxes.html.

Taxation of Social Security Benefits		
Combined income limitations for taxation of Social Security retirement benefits (1/2 Social Security + gross adjusted income + tax-free interest)		
% of taxable Social Security	Single/head of household	Married filing jointly
0%	Below $25,000	Below $32,000
Up to 50%	$25,000-$34,000	$32,000-$44,000
Up to 85%	$34,000+	$44,000+

Another thing to be cognizant of is you can continue to work while you receive Social Security benefits; if you haven't reached full retirement age and you're in this situation, you may have to deal with taxes.

Social Security Earnings Test			
Age	Amount Over Annual Income	Income Earned	Reduced Benefit
From 62 to the end of the year before FRA	$17,040	$2	$1
Calendar year in which you reach FRA	$45,360	$3	$1
Month you reach FRA	No limit	$0	$0

As you can see from the chart, if your wages are more than $17,040 (the 2018 limit), your Social Security benefits will be reduced by $1 for every $2 you earn over that limit. Before your eyes pop out, I'd like to remind you that this will only be the case for you between 62 and whatever your full retirement age is.

The year you turn FRA, the Social Security Administration will only reduce your benefits by $1 for every $3 you earn over $3,780 a month (an annual limit of $45,360). That's a much higher limit. Once you reach your full retirement age, your wages will no longer affect your Social Security payments, and the benefits that were reduced will now be added back into your Social Security calculation, netting you an even higher monthly benefit than you initially qualified for.

Final Considerations

A final point we want to make about taking your Social Security benefit has to do with those reasons to start benefits early. If you have a legacy goal, you may want to factor that into your Social Security decision. We don't mean that you have a specified lump sum goal. Instead, we mean that you may have children or a charity or someone or something in mind to whom you want to leave your assets when you pass into the next life, and your monthly Social Security check isn't something you can pass on to the next generation.

If you want to pass on as much as possible to the next generation, then you may want to consider avoiding a scenario where you're drawing down assets to avoid taking your Social Security benefit until 70. In this scenario, you're spending and living on what you could be passing on to your beneficiaries. So, a caveat to waiting to age 70 to start your Social Security benefits is that you might think about whether you're doing that at the expense of your hard-worked-for assets.

One example was a client couple of ours, let's call them Bob and Judy. They had five children, and three of their adult children for various reasons were in financial need. Leaving enough money for their adult children was a real priority for them; Bob and Judy wanted to be sure their children would be taken care of no matter what. Yet, Bob and Judy had retired at 60 and were determined to delay taking Social Security for as long as possible, hopefully until at least 66, their FRA. The couple then was alarmed when they realized that, for those six "gap" years, they would have to draw 100 percent of their retirement funding from their own saved resources. They realized, should they pass away shortly before or even after beginning Social Security, even if they had delayed their Social Security in order to get a larger monthly check, that monthly check wouldn't go to their children. And, they would have spent six years' worth of their children's inheritable assets, or at least that's how they were thinking about it.

If you take your Social Security to live on instead of withdrawing your own savings, there will be more savings to pass on in an inheritance. But delaying your Social Security benefits could net you a larger monthly check, and, should you live a long, long time, could net more in lifetime benefits. There is no single *right* way to take Social Security. There's just *right for you*. While this isn't a decision that is light, or easy to make, it can be easier if you know where your Social Security income might fit within a larger picture.

Sitting still for the picture.

CHAPTER 4

Estate Planning

Leave a legacy, not a mess.

We like to take a holistic approach at Kelly Capital Partners, and understanding your estate planning needs is essential to complete any retirement plan. Planning for what happens after your death is at the top of the list of things people hate to do. Here's a fact: There is never a convenient time to put your affairs in order. But setting up an estate plan is easy compared to how hard it can be for families to "figure it out" when they are in a state of high emotion.

No one wants to confront a jam-packed storage unit full of things. No one wants to pay a lawyer to create an estate plan. But it's important to remember that whatever **you** haven't done will be left for your family to do. Your family will not have the choice to put things off indefinitely. Your responsibilities will become theirs.

When you lose a loved one, you are left in a state of grief and emotional distress, and with that comes shock and confusion. You never want your family to be in a state like that while trying to figure out how the funeral is going to be paid for, or how the bills will be paid the next month and the months to follow. Death is agonizing enough without adding these energy drains on top of the emotional distress of your passing, along with their already busy, full lives. An estate plan that is well-thought-out and prepared by a qualified attorney in conjunction with your tax advisor and financial professional can help ensure your family is taken care of and your wishes are carried out when you are gone.

While we are on the subject of cleaning up, you will want to clean up relationship clutter: Ensure your relationships are complete. If you or someone important to you were to die today, you would want nothing left unfinished or unsaid. Do you have any relationships where that isn't currently possible?

A will can help make the transition after a loss as painless as possible for your loved ones. Your property will be transferred. Wills name individuals who will receive the specific property and describe the estate. If you have a living will, you will be able to designate the type of medical directives you wish if you are ever in a state where you can't communicate to your family or medical personnel. You can also appoint a health care power of attorney; this person will make end-of-life or medical decisions for you.

A will won't bypass probate, and an improperly drawn up will could leave your family with a mess to sort out in probate court. Probate is the process by which a court determines a will's validity, or, alternately, if there is no will, probate is the process by which a court determines how your property and assets will be split according to intestacy laws of the state where you reside. Probate means court costs, attorneys and fees, shrinking the value of your estate.

Trusts are an estate planning tool that can avoid probate altogether. Different kinds of trusts have specific uses and tax breaks and stipulations, but overall they can give you greater control of your assets, based on the specific language within the trust.

One relevant story comes to mind of our client, we will call him Steve. Steve was married with one child, Amy, who was age 9. Unfortunately, Steve met an untimely death at age 45. His wife, Patty, was, of course, completely devastated. Financially, Patty and Amy would be okay. First, Patty was an accountant with steady employment in an industry she could rely on. Also, Steve had a life insurance policy and had been diligent about maxing out his contributions to his 401(k). His will passed a sizeable amount of assets to his wife and daughter, although he hadn't used a trust.

As time went on, Patty eventually met Robert. Robert and Patty were married soon after they met. Robert struggled to stay employed and Patty was the breadwinner of the family. When Patty came in for a review, she brought Robert and directed us to change the primary beneficiary on the accounts from her and Steve's daughter, Amy, to Robert. Now, if Patty were to predecease Robert, all of the assets Steve built would transfer to Robert, potentially disinheriting Amy entirely. If Steve had taken the time to create and fund a trust with an estate planning attorney, he could have ensured his daughter was taken care of before any additional family members.

There are many different types of trusts, and any decisions you make about which type to use should be done in lockstep with an estate planning attorney. There are several advantages to trusts, depending on your needs and the trust structure. They can avoid tax burdens, manage property and avoid the costly and time-consuming burden of probate for your loved ones. Many corporations offer estate planning services to their employees through their benefits package, so that can be a good place to start for these services.

No matter where you start and how you approach these details, an estate planning attorney and competent team can be very important—if not essential—in dealing with complicated issues that can significantly impact how your assets are passed on to the people you want to have them. Let's consider, for example, the implications of the "Enhanced Life Estate Deed," commonly known as "The Lady Bird Deed."

Enhanced Life Estate Deeds

People with a knowledge of American First Ladies might recognize the reference to the wife of President Lyndon Johnson. Legend has it the Florida attorney who first wrote such a deed used members of LBJ's family to illustrate how the deed might work. In one example, he envisioned Lady Bird Johnson owning a home she wanted deeded to an heir—eventually. She didn't want to give up the home immediately, figuring she might still live in it at some point. She also wanted to be able to change her mind about selling the house or even re-deeding it to someone else.

The Lady Bird Deed, as it became known, would give Mrs. Johnson the right to live in the house—or to sell it, rent it or re-deed it—during the course of her lifetime. The property would pass to the heir, person or institution of her choice only after her death.

The Lady Bird Deed, as originally written, is used today in three states—Florida, Texas and Michigan—though 15 states recognize some form of the enhanced life estate deed. This provision allows the transfer of property without probate following a person's death. It allows the person deeding the property to continue to live in it as well as profit from it through rentals, sale or development. The beneficiary of the deed takes ownership of the property only after the death of the person who deeded it. The beneficiary inherits the property without the fees and time involved in probate court. The property transfers free of all claims by creditors and complications from lost or contested wills.

This type of deed can be used as part of a trust, but it can also be used effectively outside a trust. It is, in short, a simpler and less expensive transfer of property without having to establish a sometimes-costly trust. For many people without complicated estates—folks who have, say, a small amount of cash in bank accounts, or a single home or other simple property—the establishment of a Lady Bird Deed along with proper beneficiary designations on their bank accounts can effectively transfer assets to their heirs without using a trust.

When placed within a trust, the Lady Bird Deed can designate the trust as the recipient of the property, an option that can be helpful for those seeking or using

Medicaid to help pay for long-term nursing care or assisted living.

Note here that to qualify for Medicaid—health-related assistance for people with limited resources—one must demonstrate real need. You are generally allowed to keep a small amount of cash, one car and a home, provided it is a primary residence and is deeded in your name. Any home included in a trust, however, is considered an asset as opposed to being your primary residence. Consequently, people hoping to demonstrate limited resources in order to qualify for Medicaid assistance often have to dispose of such homes.

The Lady Bird Deed, however, allows you to continue to live in a home that is owned by the trust and is not considered your personal asset for the purpose of establishing Medicaid eligibility.

Moreover, note that all estates are required to reimburse Medicaid for payments made to patients whose probated estates suggest they had the means while living to make those payments themselves. But any home sheltered by a Lady Bird deed is not considered part of the deceased's estate—it now belongs to the designated beneficiary—when it comes to calculating the Medicaid "take back."

Keep in mind, too, that Lady Bird Deeds are not available in all states, and that different states have different rules when it comes to Medicaid eligibility and estate "take back." This is why contacting an estate planning lawyer is often an important consideration.

Plan for the Unexpected

We all hope to live long, productive lives. We envision living to normal life expectancy or beyond. Sadly, not everyone will have that opportunity, which is why proper estate planning must include looking ahead to the unpleasant prospect of an early demise.

Actor Phillip Seymour Hoffman lived a productive and celebrated life that included an Academy-Award-winning performance in "Capote." But his sudden and shocking death at age 46 resulted in a messy estate situation from which the rest of us can take lessons.

According to various media reports, Hoffman left behind an estate estimated to be worth some $35 million, only to have $15 million of it eaten up by taxes before it could be passed on to his intended heirs. A report in the New York Post indicated Hoffman had rejected the advice of his accountant to set aside money in a trust fund for his three children. He reportedly said he did not want "trust fund kids" and that his money should go directly to the children's mother, Marianne "Mimi" O'Donnell.

Hoffman, O'Donnell and their children lived as a family for most of their relationship but, because the couple never married, their home situation created estate and tax issues that many of us might prefer to avoid. Among them:

Marriage matters. Hoffman set up provisions through which O'Donnell would receive his estate, yet O'Donnell had to pay massive taxes. That's because a married person can pass on an unlimited amount to a spouse tax-free, but estate and gift taxes take a toll on a non-married couple. In Hoffman's case, every dollar of his estate over $5.34 million was subject to gift/estate taxes.

Even though Hoffman had a will, it became a messy matter of *public record in the probate court*. Not only were Hoffman's personal affairs suddenly made public, but settling his estate also became time-consuming and unnecessarily expensive. If Hoffman wanted to avoid this scenario, one possible alternative would have been establishing a revocable trust that included a simple pour-over will that titled everything to the trust. Hoffman's estate could have been settled outside the court in a far less expensive and public manner.

Hoffman *failed to update his will* to reflect the births of his youngest two children. While he had provisions for his firstborn son, his two daughters were not mentioned.

Now, did Hoffman understand that he might have passed on an additional $15 million to his life partner had they only gotten married? We'll never know.[15]

Another celebrity death offers a slightly different lesson.

When "Sopranos" star James Gandolfini died unexpectedly at age 51, published reports said some $30 million of his $70 million estate went to the IRS instead of his loved ones. Moreover, some people questioned provisions of Gandolfini's estate documents that provided

---

[15] Julia Marsh. July 21, 2014. "Philip Seymour Hoffman didn't want "trust fund kids."
https://nypost.com/2014/07/21/philip-seymour-hoffman-didnt-want-trust-funds-for-his-children/.

significant assets to his then-young daughter at the time of her 21st birthday.[16]

Certainly, some parents may believe their children will be ready to manage a considerable inheritance by age 21. Some consider a more optimum age to be 25 or 30. For many parents doing estate planning, such decisions often depend on how that parent sees a child maturing, or not.

Others choose to write incentives or inducements into wills and trusts that require young heirs to achieve certain goals in life—to finish college, for instance, or start a career—before receiving a significant inheritance. The prospect of a big payday arriving with a college diploma might be all the incentive Junior needs to hit the books more seriously.

There are limits, of course, to the strings/incentives a parent can include in a will or trust. Provisions that are clearly unreasonable—such as demanding that an heir divorce a spouse before receiving inherited money—would almost certainly be ruled invalid in court.

The bottom line here is that when you are concerned with passing on assets—no matter how big or small—an estate plan that includes at least a will if not a trust that spells out your specific intentions is essential.

---

[16] Robert W. Wood. July 20, 2013. "6 Estate Planning Lessons from James Gandolfini's Will."
https://www.forbes.com/sites/robertwood/2013/07/20/key-lessons-from-james-gandolfinis-will/.

Pat and Janie Kelly, San Diego 2017.

CHAPTER 5

The Role of Life Insurance in Retirement

"Aspire to inspire before you expire."
~Eugene Bell Jr.,
author of "What Are YOU Waiting For?"

During our working years, when careers were still developing and young families still growing, the value of life insurance might best be summarized in two words: death benefit. We purchased insurance with as much death benefit as possible for the least amount of premium, our goal being to protect a spouse or children in the event of our premature death and resulting loss of income.

Our approach to life insurance tends to change as we near or enter retirement. Now the kids are grown and may have families of their own. The concept of downsizing begins to settle in, and for many retirees that brings up the question, "Why would I still want life insurance at my advanced age?"

The answer to that question may lie in a new approach to life insurance, one that emphasizes two different words, "living benefits," in addition to death benefits.

Indeed, retirement is the time when we start thinking about living 20 years or more on something other than the weekly paychecks we counted on in our working years. It is the time we need to consider alternative income streams, or ways to finance long-term health care needs. Life insurance can be one such source.

Not that the traditional reasons to have life insurance have gone away. Retirees might still have dependent disabled adult children who need insurance protection when they no longer have parents there to help them. There might be ongoing financial obligations—perhaps a home mortgage to pay off, or past bills to pay. How will a surviving spouse handle those obligations without making a dramatic change in lifestyle?

More important, how will a surviving spouse fare financially over what could be decades following the death of a loved one? Social Security benefits suddenly are reduced from two people to one; taxes on single payers are often higher than on couples; health care costs rise as age does; and long-term nursing care becomes a bigger possibility.

This is why life insurance can play an important role in a retirement plan.

Its death benefit does what it always has done. That is, it helps surviving family members deal with immediate obligations such as funeral expenses and future financial needs, and can be a vehicle for legacy. Beyond that, "living benefits" riders—options on many of today's life insurance policies that may be available for an additional charge—allow retirees to use portions of their death benefits while still alive. Such riders can generate a monthly income stream, and some will double a monthly or annual benefit when it becomes necessary to help pay for qualified long-term care expenses.[17]

Important, too, is the way death benefits assure beneficiaries a tax-free source of income that is not subject to probate and generally not subject to estate taxes.

For all those reasons and more, retirees who consider dropping life insurance might want to reconsider, or at the very least consider a different kind of policy with the living benefits more suitable to their new situation in life.

When deciding how much life insurance is enough in retirement, some of the same conditions apply from our working years. Among those considerations: How much will your family need to cover the immediate expenses following your death—funeral expenses, medical bills, mortgage payments, paying your children's college costs, estate-settling expenses?

Now ask, how much is needed for future expenses? What will it take to keep your surviving spouse and dependents from living a drastically altered lifestyle? In short, how will your survivors replace the lost cash flow following your death?

I know a couple, we will call them Bob and Sandy, who were running their family's paint business. The business fell on hard times after 2008. Bob and Sandy both worked there, and poured everything they had into

---

[17] Elder Law Answers. June 14, 2018. "Hybrid Policies Allow You to Have Your Long-Term Care Insurance Cake and Eat It Too."
https://www.elderlawanswers.com/hybrid-policies-allow-you-to-have-your-long-term-care-insurance-cake-and-eat-it-too-15541.

this business, money and soul. Three years later, Bob became stricken with colon cancer and passed away within six months of the diagnosis. When I was talking to Sandy a year later, she said Bob let his life insurance lapse when they fell on hard times, so he could cut their monthly expenses. She expressed to me, "He did not think he was going to die." But I thought to myself, "Who ever does?" We all think we will keep on living, but the reality is not all of us live long lives. In this case, Sandy really could have benefited from that life insurance policy because they had incurred so much debt during the downturn to keep the business going.

Traditional life insurance—such as a whole life or a universal life policy—would have helped Sandy, no doubt. But there are other types of policies available today that could offer both the immediate protection she could have used at the time of her husband's death, as well as living benefits that could help her later in life.

The indexed universal life (IUL) policy provides a death benefit and the potential to build cash value that can be used while the insured is still alive.

The policy's cash value, the money you pay in premiums, has the potential to grow tax-deferred based on an external index. Similar to the way a fixed index annuity works, the money in your life insurance policy is not itself invested in the stock market, and you won't lose value due to the performance of the stock index. Yet, the insurance company agrees to credit a certain amount of interest to your policy based on the chosen market index's performance, limited by a cap, spread or percentage of that index's gains. Unlike a 401(k) or traditional

IRA, there is no limit to how much you can pay in premiums in an IUL, as well as no tax on loans you take against the policy and no required minimum distributions at age 70 ½. (Note that there is a point in which overfunding an IUL will cause it to become a Modified Endowment Contract, or a "MEC," which has tax implications you need to be aware of).[18]

In addition to paying a tax-free death benefit to a spouse, children or other designated beneficiaries, the IUL has "loan provisions"—an option to access the policy's cash value while the insured is still alive. The policy owner takes out loans against the cash value of the policy. The loans reduce the cash value and death benefit of the policy, and are tax-free if they don't exceed the amount of premiums paid. Upon the death of the insured, the loans are paid back from the death benefit. Any remaining death benefit is paid tax-free to beneficiaries.

Some index universal life insurance policies offer long-term care riders that allow a policyholder to use a percentage of the death benefit toward qualified long-term care expenses. A common industry definition of a qualifying long-term care event is that the individual is unable to perform two of the six activities of daily living.

Another insurance option for funding nursing or assisted living care is to purchase a traditional long-term-

---

[18] Policy loans and withdrawals will reduce available cash values and death benefits and may cause the policy to lapse or affect any guarantees against lapse. Additional premium payments may be required to keep the policy in force. In the event of a lapse, outstanding policy loans in excess of unrecovered cost basis will be subject to ordinary income tax. Tax laws are subject to change. You should consult a tax professional.

care insurance policy. The cost of this insurance rises as you grow older, and it is a use-it-or-lose-it proposition with no additional benefits beyond helping pay for expenses associated with long-term care. But if you can afford it, you might consider it, as the cost of a home health care aide, an assisted living facility or a nursing home can quickly deplete your retirement savings.

Following is an example of how the IUL works. This hypothetical example shows that in a year when the market index experiences a gain, the policy has the potential to earn interest tied to the index, while never being invested in the market itself. Your interest won't equal all of the gains that the market earns due to limitations such as caps, spreads or participation rates. However, you also won't lose money due to market loss in a down year. Note in this example that even when the market goes down, your policy value remains flat so that you don't have to make up for losses due to down market years. Your policy's cash value is locked in.

In the following example, the top line represents an IUL purchased with a $100,000 premium, with interest credits based on the historical performance of the S&P 500 and assuming a cap of 12.5 percent.

The second line represents the movement of the S&P 500 index itself. (Note that it is not possible to invest in the index itself).

The third line reflects the IUL assuming no interest was earned in any year, demonstrating the value of the guaranteed 0 percent interest floor. As you can see, in this worst-case scenario, even though the market had down years, your policy value never decreased due to this.

Keep in mind that this is based on historical hypothetical performance, and your actual results will vary, perhaps significantly. Past performance of the index cannot be used to predict its future performance. Life insurance involves policy fees and expenses, the amount of which varies by individual and will reduce the figures shown here. In addition, you may need to qualify for life insurance through underwriting.

IUL
Index Interest Crediting and Downside Protection

IUL Value Based on S&P 500 Index with 12.5% Cap

Annual Total Return of the S&P 500

IUL Floor Assuming 0% Interest All Years

CHAPTER 6

Risks in Retirement

"A bend in the road is not the end of the road…
Unless you fail to make the turn."
~ Helen Keller

The U.S. economy is continually changing. And perhaps at the forefront of it all, the U.S. stock markets are consistently inconstant. More than ever before, the economy and its markets intertwine with and depend upon technology. The economy changes, the markets react. And these reactions happen more quickly than ever before. For millions of American retirees and the tens of thousands of us entering or nearing retirement every day, this can be unnerving and unsettling.

Navigating quick market reactions is just one of many changes today's retirees must learn to cope with. This evolving landscape presents other risks, as well. Risks that threaten our retirement dollars and even put our retirements in jeopardy.

For instance, as we touched on in Chapter 2: The days of the defined-benefit plan are gone. In its place is the much-less-certain defined-contribution plan, such as the

401(k), in which the future retiree/investor can determine how his future retirement money is invested. It requires more hands-on management than ever before.

Those of us putting together our retirement income plans are compelled to pay closer attention to today's changing retirement environment.

One of the first risks we want to address is what we call the ***risk of reduced earnings***. This is not to be confused with the fact that our earnings are necessarily reduced when we are no longer working—that's an obvious thing, that no job equals no paycheck. Instead, the risk of reduced earnings is a risk posed to those who plan to keep working in some capacity while retired. (Semiretired, if you will.) The majority of people we talk with on a daily basis have some aspiration of working or continuing to work while retired. In other words, they aspire to retire from their full-time career, yet are hoping to work in a similar capacity or career with fewer hours, more flexibility, and the same level of pay.

Many retirees find working part-time to be vitally important to their retirement. In addition to remaining mentally sharp, socially engaged and physically fit, it provides another obvious advantage: additional cash flow and all the good that brings. And, as long as you remain actively employed, if your work place's retirement plan allows it, you don't have to take a required minimum distribution from that plan until the year you retire. This only applies to work-sponsored plans of your current employer. You still have to take required minimum distributions at 70 ½ on all other plans, such as an IRA or a plan from a previous employer.

But, beware of the drawbacks. It can complicate your financial situation. Be sure you take a long-term view of your comprehensive retirement financial plan before you agree to take a part-time job. You could end up in a higher tax bracket. If you receive Social Security, your benefits are taxable based on your provisional income. Provisional income includes wages, dividends, capital gains, retirement account distributions and 50 percent of your Social Security benefits.

Earned income can bump you up into a higher tax bracket than you planned for, for income tax, and for capital gains taxes, as well.

So, what are some of the reasons people choose to try to work in retirement?

- They simply want to ease into retirement
- They aren't fully ready to exit the workforce
- They need the income to get by/haven't saved enough money to live on
- They are pushed to retire before they wanted to, thus forced to try to find another job if they can.

Unfortunately, despite all the advantages of continuing to work even after retirement age, this isn't always an option. To underscore this point, note the following facts:[19]

---

[19] Rodney Brooks. Washington Post. March 12, 2016. "Not ready to retire, but not finding work."

- Unemployed workers 55 or older are the least likely to find another job.
- About 80 percent of late-aged workers think they'll work past retirement age.
- Only about 19 percent actually do.

Another risk we face in retirement is a ***miscalculated risk tolerance.***

Most people are familiar with the concept of risk/reward as summarized in the popular expression "nothing ventured, nothing gained." Our likelihood to take risks in the hope of realizing greater rewards changes throughout the course of a lifetime. When we are young investors, we are more likely to have a higher risk tolerance, knowing we have time to recover from the occasional market downtown. As we get closer to or enter into retirement, however, this risk tolerance generally lowers. Simply put, we can no longer assume we have 20 years or more to recover from a market downturn. Our willingness to take risks with our retirement nest egg also is typically reduced when we no longer have a steady paycheck to supplement those retirement savings.

This doesn't mean, though, that there isn't a place for some element of risk when assessing our investment portfolio in retirement. You still want some growth in the accounts from which you are now actively taking income.

---

https://www.washingtonpost.com/business/get-there/a-retirement-crisis-when-your-career-doesnt-last-as-long-as-you-expect/2016/03/11/116b2a46-e55a-11e5-b0fd-073d5930a7b7_story.html.

At the same time, as these investment accounts now represent a major source of retirement income—supplementing Social Security—retirees are understandably more conservative about their investments during the inevitable periods of stock market volatility. Some investors with investment portfolios that are more aggressive in their risk-taking approach find themselves engaged in panic-selling during market downturns. That, consequently, can turn short-term paper losses into realized losses.

This is where assessing your risk tolerance in retirement comes in. Maybe you have the resources that allow you to ride out a market downturn, much the same way you did as a younger investor. An element of moderate risk might be perfectly acceptable for you. On the other hand, if the kind of losses we saw as recently as the Great Recession of 2008 would cause you to lose sleep at night, perhaps you should avoid being exposed to any great level of risk and might want to consider a more conservative, low-risk/low-reward investment strategy.

There are many risks people have the potential to face in the retirement phase of their lifetime, that need to be addressed in their retirement plan. People need to have strategies in place to protect them against potential risks.

Everyone categorizes risk differently, but in our practice, we've catalogued half a dozen important ones. We encourage our clients to attend to these early. They can always be re-visited as time and circumstances change. But, in no particular order, here they are:

- Longevity risk
- Sequencing of returns risk

- Inflation and cost of living risks
- Stock market risk
- Liquidity risk
- Going it alone

Longevity Risk

We are living longer; consider the fact that we have more presidents alive today than there have ever been before in U.S. history. Five U.S. presidents are alive today, not counting the one in office: Jimmy Carter, George H. W. Bush, Bill Clinton, George W. Bush and Barack Obama. Thanks in part to the constant advancement of medical technology, we are living longer than our parents. Longevity risk presents a reality for most people. This is the risk of living too long and running out of money—this is the No. 1 fear of many people facing retirement today. [20]

Longevity risk is the risk every investor takes when he projects how long he is going to live. How long we live—living too long, actually—is a risk that is out of our control. But, the question is: how long are you going to PLAN for? Age 80? 90? What if you're still alive and well then? The actual length of your retirement could be much shorter—or longer—than the statistical life-expectancy imputes. So, no one can truly know how long we'll need to generate income from our assets. The most

[20] Lea Hart. Journal of Accountancy. Oct. 6, 2016. "Americans' biggest retirement fear: Running out of money."
https://www.journalofaccountancy.com/news/2016/oct/americans-fear-running-out-of-retirement-money-201615242.html.

conservative way to manage longevity risk is to plan to live to 100 and to have some sort of financial product that will account for this scenario.

Sequencing of Returns Risk

According to the "sequence of returns risk" theory, a portfolio that includes regular withdrawals could be impacted in a big way if there are negative returns in the first few years of retirement.

To explain this as simply as possible, this theory suggests that two retirees with identical initial investments and with portfolios that have identical annual returns can experience vastly different long-term outcomes, depending on when in the normal stock market cycle each person begins taking income—i.e., selling assets to generate revenue.

Consider the plight of a person who begins taking income from retirement investment accounts when they are not performing well. To generate a desired amount of income at a time when his portfolio is not performing well, this retiree must necessarily sell more shares to realize his income goal. And though the market will likely bounce back in time—as it usually does—his participation in that rebound will be reduced by the lower number of shares he has remaining in his accounts.

Conversely, a retiree who has the means to generate income without selling parts of a retirement portfolio during a market downturn will generally find a more positive long-term performance in that portfolio. Simply put, by selling investment assets when prices are higher, he can sell fewer assets to generate his income goal.

Sequence of Returns Matters

Retirement TIMING GAP between Jennifer and John is **13 YEARS**

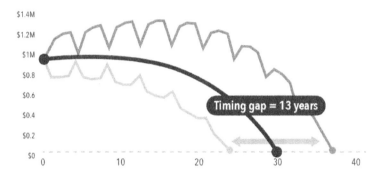

An interesting thing to note here is that both investors in the preceding hypothetical example might experience different long-term results even though the overall performance of the market is the same during, say, a 30-year history of their investment portfolio. Let's say that each person averages a conservative 6 percent growth over the same 30 years. But, the person who first started taking income when his portfolio was down finds himself in an early hole from which it is more difficult to escape, running the risk of zeroing his account somewhere near 25 years. The person who can wait until a more positive market cycle before first taking income starts out on a higher level that allows him to better survive the inevitable downturns that come later. The person whose account avoids market downturns in the first year or so may see their portfolio last closer to 40 years, in this example.

Inflation Risk

Some readers of this book might well remember a time in their teens when they could drive for a long time on $2 of gasoline. This was, of course, at a time when gas cost 25 cents a gallon. Some of these same folks likely can recall paying just $1 to see a movie—and a new release, at that.

McDonald's menu from 1972.

Those days are gone forever. Such is the effect of inflation.

Most people understand "inflation" refers to the rate at which the price of goods and services rise. One of the most commonly understood indicators of the inflation rate is the U.S. government's Consumer Price Index, which measures the rise in prices of many commonly purchased goods and services used in the typical American home.

Though the average inflation rate is low at the time this book is being written in 2018—rising at 2 percent or less from 2012 through 2017—readers here might well remember their parents worrying about "double-digit in-flation" during the 1970s. Or, perhaps they were budget-conscious wage earners themselves when inflation aver-aged between 4 ½ and 6 percent, as recently as 1987 through 1990.

Not as easily understood is why planning for inflation is an essential part of any retirement strategy.

Inflation, quite simply, eats away at the purchasing power of the money in your retirement nest egg. It seems obvious to say that the retirement assets you had in 2017 won't buy as much in 2027 and beyond, but many people fail to take this inflation factor into consideration when planning and budgeting for retirement.

This is understandable, to some extent.

That's because, in the days when we were working, employers often offered cost-of-living adjustments that likely didn't keep up with the rate of inflation, but at least partially offset it. For years, we either assumed or lived with the hope that increases in wages and compensation would keep us at least within striking distance of the rise in food, fuel and other standard costs of living.

In retirement, however, the only cost-of-living adjust-ment (COLA) we are likely to see is the small annual COLA in Social Security benefits—a hike tied to the rise in the CPI. So, our Social Security paycheck may match the rate of inflation, but what about the rest of our as-sets? This is why it is essential to make our own inflation adjustments when budgeting for retirement. Inflation is one of the few constants we can expect in retirement.

Medical costs, for instance, are generally expected to increase—likely exceeding the annual rise in the CPI—as we get older and our bodies begin to break down.

The prospect of long-term nursing care is another potential asset-depleting factor that must be considered in any long-term retirement plan. The average cost of a nursing home in the state of Michigan at the time this book is being written is close to $8,000 per month.[21] Because no one knows how long a person might need such assistance, the prospect of long-term asset depletion is considerable. Even when one spouse becomes the caregiver for the other, the expense of this can be significant.

So, how does one plan for inflation in retirement planning?

There was a time in our parents' days when simply putting money into a savings account offset much of the inflation factor. Those days of 4 to 5 percent interest rates on bank accounts are gone, however. In the extremely low-interest era following the Great Recession, a CD offering less than 1 percent interest is not keeping pace with even moderate inflation.

In a similar vein, certain types of bonds are relatively conservative and can still hold a place in a conservative retirement portfolio. Keep in mind, however, that, while most bonds pay a fixed rate of interest until their maturity date, their interest rate doesn't go up but inflation can, eroding the bond's value. While that hasn't been a major concern in recent low-inflation years, the prospect

---

[21] Genworth Financial. June 2017. "Genworth 2017 Cost of Care Survey." https://www.genworth.com/aging-and-you/finances/cost-of-care.html.

of rising interest rates in 2019 and beyond makes the relationship between inflation and bonds something to think about.

A key consideration, then, is to have some element of growth potential in a retirement portfolio.

Again, the amount of risk you care to take is up to you, and no one is suggesting you become a casino gambler when it comes to your retirement savings. At the same time, however, a person nearing or in retirement should consider some level of conservative, steady growth in their retirement investments to account for even moderate levels of inflation.

The risk that inflation and a generally higher cost of living pose to our retirement lifestyle are pretty simple: What we spend today to live our life simply isn't going to be adequate five years from now … 10 years from now … or 15 years from now. Even if we assume we will be doing exactly what we do now and buying only what we currently buy, the $4,000 a month you live on today simply won't go as far in a dozen years.

Over time, inflation erodes the purchasing power of every dollar. It doesn't require hyper-inflation, either. Even low inflation will have an impact on long-term purchasing power. So, the question becomes, how do we respond correctly to inflation in our retirement budgeting? We need a plan that adjusts for inflation over time.

- Make necessary inflation adjustments.
- Increase your monthly payouts incrementally to account for inflation.

Even risk-averse people may want to consider having some money invested for growth to help keep up with inflation and personal spending. Guaranteed, principal-protected accounts simply might not keep up with inflation in today's low-interest return environment.

Stock Market Risk

During our working years as we were putting aside money in qualified accounts, many of us relied heavily on stocks or equities for long-term growth opportunity. Retirement is generally the time to reduce investment risk. Bear markets and unfavorable sequences of returns happen. So, when a broker or advisor presents a financial plan to you, pay close attention to what kind of assumptions they are making about the future. Most financial models use an "assumed rate of return." Be careful of projected future growth. Many things affect this, such as:

- How much are you withdrawing from the portfolio?
- What is the inflation assumption?
- If you're presented a model with an assumed rate of return of 6–8% across your portfolio, what will you do in years the market fails to deliver? Will you choose to turn off your income withdrawal altogether? Or will you choose to reduce the amount you withdraw?
- How much risk do you need to expose your assets to in order to achieve an average 7%

return? What is the standard deviation on the
risk bell curve in trying to reach that return?

A good question to ask yourself is, if I retire, how
much stock should I have in my retirement accounts?
The answer varies for everyone. With the bull market for
stocks nearing a decade old, many advisors say it's time
to adjust equity allocations. But it depends on individual
situations. Nothing should be done without talking with
a professional first. Some investors, particularly those
near retirement, may want to consider reducing the risk
their portfolio is exposed to. Middle-aged investors seeking to preserve some of their portfolio after the bull run
might have a different strategy. Younger investors have
the benefit of time on their side and can afford to be
more aggressive with their portfolio.

Tolerance for market risk can mean different things
to different people—so, emotionally, if a person is taking on more risk than they can tolerate, then their emotions get involved and they may be more inclined to
panic and sell.

In the context of investing, you need to understand
your personal tolerance for risk. An aggressive investor
is willing to risk losing money for the potential of better
results. This means risking a reduction to your standard
of living in exchange for the potential of growing your
nest egg. A more conservative investor would prefer to
focus on preserving their nest egg and current lifestyle.
When we put it this way, it tends to take on a whole new
meaning.

I suggest people understand the level of earnings
they'll need to support their lifestyles in retirement.

- How much will Social Security provide?
- How much will pensions provide?
- How much is needed over and above that?
- Are withdrawals from savings and investments sustainable over time?
- If it's not enough, how much can be realistically earned from a job?
- Is that job reliable for the long term?
- How long can a person physically stay employed?

Emergency Expenses

The next risk we need to account for before we enter into retirement is emergency expenses, known as liquidity risk. Many people tend to forget to plan for unpredictable or emergency expenses. Be sure of this: They will befall you. They befall us all from time to time. We need to have a plan, something in place where we can access additional money when we need it to pay for unforeseen things. This is liquid money we can get to easily and quickly, money that is not exposed to volatility when you need to withdraw it. Here are some of the situations that can arise:

- Divorce
- Changes in tax laws
- Changes in health care costs
- Helping family members
- Long-term illness
- Long-term care

- Home maintenance or repairs
- Auto upkeep, repair or replacement

This is money we can get to when we need it and it is not exposed to the ups and downs of the stock market. The task for this money is not growth, it's liquidity. To manage the risk of the unexpected before it arises we must set up something separate and aside from our expense budget and investment plan. An expense and income plan can—and will—help us pay the bills each month. But, this piece of the retirement strategy details what you will do when the roof needs to be replaced or your son or daughter comes calling for help with some reasonable-sounding expense. (Say, a down payment for a home, for instance.)

Navigating the Retirement Risks: Don't Go It Alone

So, how can you best prepare yourself for the unexpected or guard yourself against the seen and unforeseen drains on your retirement savings?

Well, you're certainly free to do it yourself, to study and educate yourself to the point that you create your own carefully constructed retirement plan with an income strategy that includes provisions for each of these risks. Some people do this with reasonable success.

They are often the exception to the rule, however.

For most other people with concerns about their quality of life during retirement, working with a financial professional is important. This is the case mainly because of the different challenges we face in retirement, elements of living we didn't routinely encounter in our working years and with which we likely have little to no expertise.

For example: Even people who did quite well in handling their own retirement investment strategies sometimes experience problems when it comes time to turn those investment assets into retirement income. This transition from the accumulation phase (when we work, save and invest to grow a retirement nest egg) to the distribution phase (when we begin taking income from those accumulated assets) can be challenging. Mistakes in turning assets into income can lead to not having enough cash to cover unexpected expenses, to incurring higher-than-necessary tax bills on retirement income, or the dreaded prospect of living longer than your money does.

Moreover, there are times when we find an investment purchased earlier in life no longer suits our needs in retirement.

I had a friend, Nancy, who was 58, single, and had no children. She was an independent sales rep and she did not have a 401(k). Her business had taken a few hits over the years, and times had been tough on occasion, but otherwise she made a nice living for herself. Her one concern was that she had a variable annuity and she was concerned about the fees she was paying on this annuity.

She arranged to meet with her agent to ask about the annuity and find out about the amount and the type of fees she was paying. The agent she had met with originally had moved on to another firm, so her original firm passed her on to another agent. Nancy discovered she was paying 3.75 percent in fees every year on her account value, which was $200,000. That was close to $8,000 in fees a year! A large portion of her returns were being eaten up in fees, meaning the market had to do very well for her to be able to make any money on her account, and in years that the market experienced setbacks, her high fees meant her setbacks set her even further back.

She questioned the rep about the types of fees she was paying, and discovered one of the fees was for a substantial death benefit. For some people, this might be appropriate, but she was a single woman with no children, and this was more or less her only retirement asset. Her intent and purpose for this money was to make sure she had enough to last her through retirement, not to leave to someone else. As she reviewed the fees and other contract terms, Nancy was shocked. We asked the agent why the contract had such an unnecessarily large death benefit that she was paying extra for, and the agent responded, "Well, when the original agent gave her the paperwork, she named two beneficiaries." Well yes, when asked who she wanted to leave her money to, she was able to name two people. That is very different from having a specific legacy goal for which you are willing to pay an additional chunk in fees.

Scenarios such as this can compound all the other risks we must face in retirement. Many people don't understand products. Likely, the original agent had told her the product had an optional death benefit that she could pass on to two people, and Nancy named two people. Instead, an agent should assess if a substantial death benefit is in someone's interest and fits their goals in the first place.

The risk of a DIY retirement can mean forgetting to account for the concrete retirement risks I named before, from illness to emergencies. It's important that you work with a financial professional you can truly trust, who can help you figure out which risks pose the biggest threat to your retirement and how to take them on.

CHAPTER 7

Taxes

"It's not how much you make,
it's how much you keep."
~ Robert Kiyosaki

A h taxes. The patriotic duty of every citizen. We should strive to pay every cent of our tax obligation—no less ... but also no more.

We often hear about the tax burden we're currently facing, but did you know that, even prior to the tax bill that takes effect this year, we were already in one of the lowest tax environments of the last century? During the last two years of World War II, the highest marginal tax bracket reached 94 percent! Even through the 1960s, the top tax tier was between 70 and 90 percent.[22]

I don't have a crystal ball to know what taxes could do in the future, but with the never-ending government

---

[22] Tax Policy Center. March 22, 2017. "Historical Highest Marginal Income Tax Rates."
https://www.taxpolicycenter.org/statistics/historical-highest-marginal-income-tax-rates.

spending and the incredible debt the nation has accumulated, I think it's fair to say there's a chance our taxes could increase in the future.

In 2015, 81 percent of each tax dollar that came into the U.S. Treasury went to pay for five things: Social Security, health programs (Medicaid, Medicare, health subsidies), national defense, social safety net programs, and interest on the national debt. As boomers finish their exit from the workforce and take their due from entitlement programs, they are no longer putting money into Social Security and Medicare but are taking money out. So, do you think the costs of those big-ticket items—especially Social Security, health and social safety net programs—are going to decrease? No. To top it off, that year, almost 15 percent of the national budget came from bonds the government sold to other countries and individuals, a.k.a. debt, which, in turn, increased the amount that future generations will spend on that "interest on the national debt" line item. This also means there is less and less available to pay for all the other things the federal government is responsible for, such as:[23]

- Disaster relief
- IRS
- Environmental Protection Agency
- National Parks Service

---

[23] Center on Budget and Policy Priorities. March 4, 2016. "Policy Basics: Where Do Our Federal Tax Dollars Go?"
https://www.cbpp.org/research/federal-budget/policy-basics-where-do-our-federal-tax-dollars-go.

- Infrastructure
- Centers for Disease Control
- Congress
- And on and on

If Congress acts to change this, there will likely be either huge cuts in benefits or massive tax hikes. If Congress does nothing, that, too, may have enormous consequences.

So, what does this looming tax cloud mean for you?

If you are like most retirees, you probably put most of your retirement assets into qualified, tax-deferred plans, the most common being the traditional IRA, 401(k) or 403(b).

Investing your money in tax-deferred retirement plans while you are working is an excellent way to save. For one thing, any money invested in these plans (up to the annual limit) is done on a pre-tax basis, meaning whatever money you invest is not subject to income tax in the year you invest it. For another, many employers make a matching contribution—sometimes up to half the amount of the employee contribution—though they are not obligated to do so. Moreover, the investment growth in the account also is not taxable until the time you begin taking income from the account.

But as there is no such thing as a free lunch, Uncle Sam will eventually want to get a (tax) bite of the money you've been sheltering from taxes all these years.

In general practice, Uncle Sam starts getting his taste when we retire and start taking income distributions from the IRA or 401(k) assets that have been growing tax-deferred all these years. Such distributions are taxed as ordinary income on both principal (the money you invested while working) and the investment growth. In theory, you may be in better position to afford these taxes in retirement because you are no longer receiving a weekly paycheck and will be—again, in theory—in a lower tax bracket.

There are, however, ways to receive tax-free income in retirement, and you need to consider these in your retirement planning.

The Roth IRA is one of the most common of the tax-free strategies. Contributions made to the Roth—typically during your working years—are made on an after-tax basis. This means you don't get the upfront tax deduction you would from a contribution to a traditional IRA or 401(k). The tradeoff is that you pay no tax when taking distributions from the Roth IRA. Because you've already paid tax on the money before it went into the Roth, the principal you invested is your money to withdraw anytime you need it without paying tax or penalty. Note, however, that special rules apply to any investment growth within the Roth account, which can incur a 10 percent tax penalty and ordinary income tax when withdrawn less than five years after opening the Roth account and before age 59 ½.

Roth IRAs are especially appealing to people who think their tax bracket might be greater in retirement than it was in their working years, which can happen if the government increases income taxes, your income increases in retirement, or as we begin to lose many of the deductions we had in our younger years—children, mortgage interest, etc. Roth IRAs are equally attractive to people of all income levels who can foresee the advantage of tax-free income in retirement.

You can begin making contributions to a Roth IRA at any age if you have taxable compensation—yes, even after retirement as a means of tax-free investment growth—although there are limits to who can contribute, and how much can be contributed in a year. Under IRS rules in place in 2018, single or head of household filers with a modified adjusted gross income (MAGI) of less than $135,000 could contribute to a Roth IRA. The income limit in 2018 is $199,000 for a married couple filing jointly.

Note, too, that any kind of investment vehicle can be employed within a Roth IRA—stocks, bonds, etc. all can realize tax-free investment growth, assuming the Roth IRA holder offers them. Such tax-free growth within the Roth gives an investment the potential to produce greater spending power (when converted into income) than might the same taxable asset held within a traditional IRA or 401(k).

Always Consider the Tax Implications

As taxes represent one of the biggest drains on a typical retirement nest egg—usually ranking only behind medical expenses for most people—a person in retirement simply must take taxes into consideration before withdrawing money from an investment portfolio.

In general, a common strategy is to first take money from taxable accounts—typically, any brokerage accounts upon which you already are paying taxes on dividends (from stocks or mutual funds) or interest (from bonds or bond funds). Turning these taxable assets into income usually involves a capital gains tax, which occurs when selling an asset for more than you paid for it. Keep in mind, however, that capital gains are taxed at a considerably lower rate than are distributions taken from tax-deferred IRAs or 401(k)s, which are taxed as ordinary income. Using this strategy, for a while, at least, your tax-deferred assets can continue to grow until you must begin taking fully taxable required minimum distributions (RMDs) at age 70 ½. We'll talk about RMDs in more detail later in this chapter.

Another strategy is to take withdrawals from different kinds of accounts, reaching a desired income goal by mixing and matching taxable and tax-free distributions with a careful eye on how these distributions affect your total taxable income. The idea here is to avoid at all costs the prospect of being elevated into a higher tax bracket.

You might, for example, drain down your tax-deferred IRA by taking only enough withdrawals—taxed as ordinary income—without being elevated into the next tax bracket. Or, if you need more income to meet your goal but are near the top of a tax bracket, you can take tax-free withdrawals from a Roth IRA, or even distributions from a taxable brokerage account—from which you've already been taxed—to avoid the unwelcome elevation into a higher tax bracket.

If you absolutely must take income from taxable brokerage accounts to meet an income goal, here are some strategies that can minimize the tax impact.

Consider first selling assets that have decreased in value, giving you a capital loss that can offset some of the capital gains you may have realized from other sales.

IRS rules in place in 2018 allow a taxpayer to use capital losses to offset the tax on capital gains, for up to a net (gains minus losses) loss of $3,000. Note also that any capital losses that exceed the $3,000 limit in any one year can be carried over into future tax years.

When considering the prospect of using capital losses to offset capital gains, first consider using short-term losses—declines in the value of any asset you've held for less than one year—to offset short-term capital gains. The idea here is to decrease your short-term capital gains as much as possible as they are taxed as ordinary income. Long-term capital gains, on the other hand, are taxed at a lower rate.

If possible, consider using cash as opposed to selling taxable assets to meet an emergency income need.

If there are no capital losses to be realized, think about selling assets with long-term capital gains before you do those with short-term gains. Once again, the reasoning here is that long-term gains are taxed at a lower rate than short-term gains, which are taxed as ordinary income.

Minimize Your Retirement Tax Obligation

We accept as a fact of life in our working years that we will be paying income tax on the wages we make. Don't imagine for a second that this obligation disappears in retirement, though there are some significant differences.

For most people in retirement, income is produced through two primary sources: Social Security and distributions from retirement investments such as IRAs,

401(k)s and other accounts. Income from retirement accounts is treated the same as wage income was in our working years—it is taxed as ordinary income. Distributions from a Roth IRA or Roth 401(k) are tax-free.

The good news, however, comes in the taxation of Social Security, which for some lucky people is tax-free. But even the wealthiest of Americans pays a tax on no more than 85 percent of Social Security benefits, meaning 15 percent is tax free.

A challenge in retirement income planning is to develop plans that keep the Social Security tax obligation as low as possible.

Let's look first at the special rules that determine how much of your Social Security benefits are taxable.

As discussed in Chapter Three, the tax owed on Social Security benefits is based on a recipient's combined income, also known as "provisional income." This amount includes everything that goes into determining the adjusted gross income figure we calculate on an annual tax return—wages, self-employment income, dividends and interest from investments, pension and annuity payments, the taxable portion of IRA distributions, rental income, alimony and any other source of taxable income.

Here I'd like to underscore that several other components also are added to determine provisional income. Any interest you receive from municipal bonds—amounts which are tax exempt for federal income tax purposes—are included in provisional income. So too is one-half of all Social Security benefits you as an individual, or you and a spouse for a married couple filing jointly, received in the tax year in question.

One final note here. These thresholds are not indexed for inflation, which makes them different from many other thresholds in the tax code. An increase in any aspect of provisional income—whether wages or IRA distributions or any other factor—can produce a kind of double whammy in taxation. Not only will the taxpayers pay a corresponding rise in normal income tax, but they might also see an increase in Social Security taxation that adds onto their overall tax bill.

The Bite of RMDs

Remember all that money that has been growing tax-deferred in an IRA, 401(k) and other qualified retirement plans? Well, Uncle Sam hasn't forgotten about it, even if you haven't given it a lot of thought. He wants to start getting a tax bite from those savings eventually, and he's determined that age 70 ½ is the age at which it is finally time to pay the piper.

It is at this age that Uncle Sam requires you to begin taking an annual percentage from the balance of all your remaining qualified (tax-deferred) accounts. This doesn't mean you have to take something from every account, but you must take a minimum distribution amount that reflects all accounts. The penalty for not doing so is severe—a 50 percent additional penalty based on the RMD amount you should have withdrawn but didn't.

Let's add here that your RMD, calculated as a percentage of your account, grows each year as you age. He wants what he considers his share of the money you've not yet paid taxes on, and he knows you're running out of time in which to pay it. Keep in mind also that any remaining tax-deferred money passed on to a following generation will include an immediate tax obligation to them.

Note too how this distribution you are required to take—whether you want it or not—becomes a factor in your provisional income calculation that affects how much you could owe in Social Security tax.

This is why you and your advisor or CPA should plan for the tax impact of RMDs and consider ways of reducing your pool of tax-deferred assets before the RMDs kick in. There are several strategies to do this, the most common of which is the Roth IRA conversion.

The Roth Conversion

The idea here, as suggested before, is to strategically begin moving assets from a tax-deferred IRA or other employer-based retirement accounts into a Roth IRA in which you will never pay tax on any future distribution.

There is a fly in the ointment, so to say. That is, you will pay tax on all money you move in any tax year from a traditional tax-deferred IRA into a Roth IRA. Again, this is Uncle Sam getting what he considers his share of taxes you've yet to pay on your retirement savings.

This is the primary reason that Roth conversions aren't for everyone. You need to be able to pay the taxes due, you want to avoid the conversion pushing you into a higher tax bracket. Also you want to assess whether your tax bracket might be higher or lower in retirement, or if you are in a five-year holding period that might make the conversion unnecessarily costly.

At the same time, however, there are several advantages in building up a Roth IRA that should be considered; advantages that, over the long term, can offset the temporary sting of paying taxes on money moved from a traditional IRA to a Roth IRA.

The money now inside the Roth can continue to grow tax-free in any investment vehicle of your choosing. And because you can now withdraw it tax-free—having already paid taxes on it either before you invested in the Roth or in the conversion process—that money will have additional spending power when you eventually take a distribution from the Roth.

Roth IRA distributions are not a component of the provisional income formula used to determine how much of your Social Security benefits can be taxed. Remember, distributions from traditional IRAs are included in provisional income. Roth IRA distributions, however, can be taken without impacting the taxation of Social Security benefits.

Roth IRA distributions are not subject to RMDs. You can hold onto your Roth assets for as long as you wish, using them only when needed.

Any money remaining in a Roth IRA at the time of the account holder's death can be passed tax-free to an heir or designated beneficiary.

The question of timing for an IRA conversion needs to be considered; conventional wisdom holds that if the purpose of a Roth conversion is to minimize taxes on Social Security, it is better to make conversions before the prospective retiree begins taking Social Security benefits. This is because any distribution from a traditional IRA—such as a conversion to a Roth IRA—figures into the provisional income formula that affects Social Security taxation. When conversions are done before a person begins receiving benefits, the only impact is on the taxpayer's taxable income for the year(s) in which the conversion is done.

Conversely, a single retiree or retired couple may already have a provisional income that exposes the maximum 85 percent of Social Security benefits to taxation.

For people in that circumstance, a Roth conversion can make sense at any time. They already pay taxes on the highest allowable amount of their benefits; any rise in provisional income isn't going to change that. The other advantages of building up a Roth IRA—passing money to heirs on a tax-friendly basis, perhaps—might be a compelling reason for making a Roth conversion if the conversion doesn't push them into a higher income-tax bracket.

Keep in mind, too, that the rules governing Roth IRAs have been known to evolve over the years. Who's to say the rules governing future years will be as helpful as the ones in place today?

Death and Taxes

It hardly seems right, but it's a fact of, well, death.

What we're talking about here is the sad realization that the passing of a spouse often means higher taxes on the survivor, even as the survivor's overall income decreases.

This happens because the survivor, long accustomed to paying taxes as part of a married couple filing jointly, suddenly is a single filer looking at income thresholds relatively lower than those known during years as a couple.

For example, a December 2014 Retirement Report from Kiplinger uses an Indiana couple:[24]

"For 2012, the year the husband died, the widow was able to file a joint return. The couple's adjusted gross income was $91,000 and their taxable income was $66,000, which fell within the 15 percent tax bracket for joint filers ($17,400 to $70,700 in 2012). Her federal tax tab: $8,884. (AGI is total income less a few adjustments, while taxable income is AGI less personal exemptions and deductions.)

"In 2013, the wife's AGI dropped to $88,000. But her taxable income rose to $69,000, as a result of losing one personal exemption and of lower medical deductions. Her taxable income bumped her into the 25 percent tax bracket for single filers ($36,250 to $87,850). Her federal tax bill: $13,365. 'If she was still married,' [her financial advisor] says, 'they would have been at the top of the 15 percent bracket.' That bracket topped out at $72,500 in 2013.

"As a single person, the widow would likely be required to pay income-related surcharges for Medicare Part B and Part D for the first time—about $640. (The trigger point for married couples is twice as high, AGI of $170,000 versus $85,000 for singles.)"

---

[24] Susan B. Garland. Kiplinger's Retirement Report. December 2014. "Plan for a Bigger Tax Bite When Spouse Dies."
https://www.kiplinger.com/article/taxes/T037-C000-S004-plan-for-a-bigger-tax-bite-when-spouse-dies.html.

Again, these increases come even with only a slight decrease in overall income and expenses. Investment income, for instance, is not likely to change with the death of a partner. Major expenses such as property taxes and maintenance costs on the family home are likely to remain the same. Yet, the simple change in tax filer status, coupled with the loss of one personal exemption, can easily elevate the surviving spouse into a higher tax bracket with an increase in taxes that is difficult to manage in the stressful time following the death of a loved one.

The so-called "widow's penalty" also leaves the surviving spouse more vulnerable to paying taxes on a higher percentage of the remaining Social Security benefit.

There are any number of things a couple can do to reduce the tax bite on a surviving spouse. Generally, these are things a couple should consider as part of a retirement income plan drawn up while both are still alive.

Converting money from a traditional IRA to a Roth IRA is one feasible strategy to help a surviving spouse avoid a potentially costly jump into a higher tax bracket following the death of a partner.

A couple in a 25 percent tax bracket, for example, might make several Roth conversions over a multi-year period, moving as much money as possible without being elevated from the 25 percent bracket. After several years of such conversions, the Roth IRA account could be at a point where a surviving spouse, who suddenly needs additional income but faces the prospect of moving into a costly higher tax bracket, can supplement income taken from taxable IRAs with tax-free distributions from a Roth IRA. By carefully balancing the two sources of income, the survivor is more likely to remain in a more familiar and favorable tax bracket.

Another option to consider, while both partners are alive and healthy enough to do so, is the purchase of life insurance, something not everyone cares to consider in retirement. Yet life insurance can produce both tax-free living benefits as well as death benefits to a survivor. Moreover, the survivor might consider using some or all of those benefits to pay the tax necessary when making any future Roth IRA conversions, or use the money to pay the tax bill should the survivor unavoidably be bumped into a higher tax bracket.

My sisters and my mom at her birthday.

CHAPTER 8

Protection, Income, Growth and Liquidity

"Money does not come with instructions."
~ Max Horne

What do you *really* want your money to do for you? There are four buckets toward which you allocate your money in retirement: protection, income, growth and liquidity.

We have talked about the idea that each individual vehicle or product is not as important as what it accomplishes and how it fits in the overall plan. So, to give you an example, let's look at how these different areas of protection, income and growth might affect the asset allocations for someone with, say, $1 million, for a nice round figure. So, first and foremost, they might look to establish some guaranteed, liquid money. In that bucket, they'd put maybe $100,000 in cash, cash equivalents, money that isn't at risk, a rainy-day fund for if they have a leak in the roof or need a new car. This can be savings and checking accounts, money market accounts.

After this, we'll turn toward our income. Now, Social Security and any pension will be obvious sources of income. So, if our hypothetical person has done that B-word exercise (psst…*budget!*) they know how much money they need coming in every month. They add their expected Social Security and pension income and determine they will still need about $3,000 of income each month. So, of the beginning $1 million, they'll put aside maybe $500,000 in vehicles for income such as alternative investments, dividend-paying stocks and certain types of annuities. Now, some of those are subject to market risk, so they likely won't put all $500,000 in the same place. Instead, at least some of the money might be in products that have contractual guarantees.

That leaves $400,000 of the original $1 million that they can position for growth potential, meaning they can invest in stocks, bonds and exchange-traded funds, as examples. Now, it is imperative that our hypothetical millionaire is in a position to separate their income and guaranteed funds from their growth funds. This barrier is to help keep people safe from emotional investing— allowing market-based assets time to grow while allowing retirees to focus on the income and liquidity that they may need immediately.

So, although we position our assets in these different areas, we still run into this "winner-takes-all" attitude in the industry, where the annuity and insurance companies will argue you should only buy insurance products, and brokerage firms will only argue that you will make more money if you don't tie your money up in insurance, and that you should buy stock instead.

But the only way to have the rainy-day money you need, income that is contractually guaranteed, AND growth opportunity that has the potential to keep up with inflation, is by using multiple products from across the spectrum. At Kelly Capital Partners we work with all the options available because we see the role each can play. We are independent, so we are not tied to any single bank, brokerage house or insurance company. To us, it is not so much about the tools as it is about the overall plan. We have all the tools necessary, and if a tool fits with the objective of the client, we will use it! We examine our options, but the main objective is always the client's objective.

But, first, let's personalize this: Whether you know it or not, when you or anyone invests in a certain product, you are investing with the hope that the vehicles you choose will deliver one or more of these benefits. Before we explore the various kinds of options out there, let's focus on the four benefits a financial asset can deliver. A consumer needs to know what to look for from each one.

Growth Opportunity

If I ask you what you really want your money to do for you, you are going to say, "Well, I want it to grow!" Right? However, any and all growth-based products will carry risk along with that growth potential. As a rule, the greater the growth potential, the greater the risk. So, when you're making investment choices, be sure you realize these two features go hand-in-hand.

Protection

Most certainly the next thing you might say is you want your money to grow, but you also don't want to lose it. You want to make it last, or you want it to be protected! The idea of "I want my cake and I want to eat it, too!" can come to mind here. Understand that growth and liquidity expectations must be kept in check when protection is a priority for your money.

Income

For those who are getting ready to retire or already retired, you might need some income from your investments as well. The first question might be, do you need income now, or at some point in the future? Then the question might be, how much do you need? How far do things like pensions, Social Security or any other source of income go?

Liquidity

We all know we might need our money randomly, or for an emergency type of purpose, so the liquidity of our money can be very important as well, and not all financial products have great liquidity access once you have stashed your money inside, so pay attention to the overall liquid access each vehicle offers. I want to talk about two different types of liquidity. Some vehicles are "fully" liquid, and others are "conditionally" liquid. By this, I mean there are some financial vehicles where you can move your money in and out at your discretion, with minimal thought to fees or taxes. Other vehicles, like some real estate investment trusts, can tie up your money for periods of time. For instance, withdrawing cash from an annuity contract before age 59 ½ could result in a 10 percent tax penalty and fines and, if money is withdrawn during the early years of a contract, a surrender charge may apply.

Let's say we have a hypothetical client named Sam who was very good about putting money in his qualified accounts, so almost all of his assets were in IRAs, 401(k)s and Roth IRAs. Sam was passionate about helping his son with his college loans. The problem was, Sam was not able to withdraw out of his IRA without incurring a 10 percent early withdrawal tax penalty because he was under 59 ½. The IRS does allow a person, however, to withdraw early out of an IRA for college tuition (at an ordinary income tax rate) as long as it goes directly to the college in order to qualify. Sam did not know this rule before his son took out a student loan, and so Sam was unable to help him. It is very important to know how the different qualifications by the IRS can have an impact on your liquidity.

Now, some people may prioritize one of the principles I've introduced but, in reality, most people need some level of all of the above items. Of course, it would be great to have one awesome vehicle that fills all of these goals. Unfortunately, no single vehicle exists. With each vehicle, you must be willing to relinquish some features in order to benefit from others. To figure out that balance, we have to answer questions about how much money we need for protection, liquidity and growth potential, all with the goal of one day providing income.

What portion of your money should be set aside for short-term needs? What about long-term planning for retirement?

Bank Products

This is the financial option we likely first learned as older children or young adults when we opened our first bank accounts and were pleased to soon learn of this thing called "interest" that allowed our accounts to grow (ever so slightly) even when we didn't make deposits.

Well, those days of meaningful growth through interest in our checking and savings account are little more than distant memories in the post-Recession days of next-to-nothing interest rates. Even certificates of deposit—which were great for our parents in the high-interest days of the 1980s and 90s—offer minimal interest as an insured deposit these days. As you probably know, bank deposits are insured by the FDIC up to specified limits.

Yet, we still maintain our bank accounts, and with good reason. Life comes at you fast. That's why most financial advisors recommend cash reserves of somewhere between six to 12 months of your cost-of-living to cover both planned and unexpected expenses. Money in our checking and savings account remains safe and liquid; we have access to it whenever we need it. CDs remain safe even though the interest is minimal. You generally have to tie up your money for longer periods of time in order to get more than a 1 percent interest rate.

The challenge all conservative consumers face is the fact that we are in a very low interest-rate environment. This means many conventional financial vehicles such as interest-bearing bank accounts, government bonds and bank CDs may not generate sustainable, lifetime retirement income.

The buying power of those dollars just is not keeping up with inflation. If you have your money in CDs and money markets just sitting in savings earning very little to no return at all, the buying power of those dollars just isn't keeping up with inflation. We just want to make sure we have a proper balance between protection, growth and liquidity so all the risks are addressed. We certainly don't want you stuffing your money in the mattress.

Investing

At the other end of the spectrum is investing. This type of money is intended for growth and usually involves a lot of liquidity, having the ability to move money in and out of the market. Many of you use these vehicles to grow your retirement savings, especially when you are younger. Since the two main features of this type of money are growth potential and liquidity, you live with the understanding that these investments are not protected or guaranteed since the market has inherent risk, which you accept.

I'd like to explain the most common investment choices found within stock and bond markets. The term "stock market" is generally used to refer to different markets and exchanges where securities are bought and sold. Examples of these are common and preferred stocks issued by both domestic and foreign companies, exchange-traded mutual funds, exchange-traded real estate investment trusts, bonds, commodities and other types of securities.

People invest in stocks for numerous reasons. Before I returned to work, I should have invested in medical supplies just to get a return on my money.

Jack, one week after we brought home the trampoline. Should have seen that one coming.

With four boys, it seemed like I was at the hospital about once a month for the most ridiculous injuries—like when Sean tried to jump off the porch one January, hurdling three steps and landing on a patch of ice. Our young daredevil landed on his head and needed staples for that one.

Truly, we should have taken out stock in staples at the very least. Charlie was the first of the boys to get them when he was zealously building a fort and swung his hammer so far back that he got the back of his own head with the hammer's claw.

Seriously, if you are investing in stocks, your primary reason should be for growth or capital appreciation. There are secondary reasons as well, among them being the liquidity of stocks. That is, if you suddenly need money, you can always sell as much of your stock holdings as necessary, taking either a profit or loss depending on the stock price at the time of the sale.

Many stocks also provide a level of income or liquidity through their monthly, quarterly or annual dividend payments. The dividends can be used to buy additional shares of the stock—called reinvesting the dividend—or the dividend can be taken directly as cash. Dividends are never guaranteed, but a stock with a steady history of paying dividends—a set price per share as determined by the company issuing the stock—is the kind of equity you might consider if you are looking for income through stock dividends.

Another way to invest in stocks, bonds and other securities—with all their inherent ups and downs—is through the purchase of mutual funds or exchange-traded funds (ETFs).

Mutual funds and ETFs are portfolios that own individual securities such as stocks and bonds. These investments allow you to own shares in a mutual fund or ETF and each share represents a portion of the fund's holdings. As is the case with common stock ownership, growth opportunity as well as income potential and liquidity are the primary reasons for ownership here. Many people believe (not necessarily accurately) that mutual funds—a "basket" of various stocks with something in common (such as utilities, health care, technology stocks, growth stocks, value stocks and so on)— have a greater degree of stability because they are professionally managed. Such management is not free, as most mutual funds contain a management fee. (ETFs, which also comprise a "basket" of stock with a common theme, do not have the higher management fees of mutual funds, making them cheaper to own.) But while there is some comfort in owning shares of a professionally managed fund, these funds rise and fall in value on a daily basis in lockstep with the stocks that make up the fund or the ETF. Remember, there is no such thing as protection or guarantees in the ownership of any stock, mutual fund or ETF.

Your primary reason for a mutual fund is still growth potential, but they may offer some liquidity as long as the fund does not have an early redemption fee or penalty. They may also pass on some dividend income depending on the fund. If you own a mutual fund you do not have protection. The words diversification and protection must be used separately!

Then there is the bond market. Bonds are not traded on an exchange like stocks. They have their own market (often, when we say "the market," we mean a collection of bond markets, stock markets and all sorts of exchanges). Bonds are used primarily for income and/or conservative growth, secondarily for some level of protection depending on the type of bond you own.

People may believe bonds might be protected because they are less volatile than stocks. However, the only bonds that are considered truly stable are government-based bonds or Treasurys, since they are backed by the U.S. Treasury Department. All other bonds (corporate, junk or municipal bonds, high-yield, etc.), can lose value and carry significant interest rate risk. These products cannot be called safe. You would purchase a bond for the income it might provide and for growth opportunity.

Something to consider when buying bonds is bonds are inverse of interest rates, so when interest rates are falling (like they did over the past 20 years) bond prices tend to go up, but it's the opposite when interest rates rise. If you sell your bond before maturity, you may make a profit or a loss, depending on the current interest rate environment and any changes in the bond's credit rating. If you don't want to own individual bonds, there are bond mutual funds similar to stock mutual funds. With bond mutual funds there is no maturity date for you to get back to "par," or the face value of the bond. Instead, you hold the fund shares for "perpetual duration." Just like individual bonds, bond funds are subject to interest rate risk. When current interest rates rise, the value of the bonds in the bond fund's portfolio often decline and thus the value of the bond fund's shares will go down. Conversely, when interest rates go down, the value of the fund's shares generally increase.

Life Insurance, Long-Term Care Insurance, Annuities

When we're looking to the long-term, we're looking at when we're approaching retirement or are already retired. That's when you're moving from the accumulation phase of your life to the preservation and distribution phase. In most cases, you don't want to subject your retirement nest egg to excessive market volatility or risk, so a key consideration is protection. Long-term money generally focuses on stability to generate income for the rest of your retirement and growth potential to hedge against inflation. Long-term investments might also provide for your long-term care needs and it might possibly establish a legacy for heirs or a favorite charity. Of course, when planning for the future, you want to consider minimizing your tax liabilities to avoid taxes where legally possible. Along with your investment objectives and income needs, you may consider how life insurance and annuities may play a part in your overall plans.

Life insurance is not an investment, but it may play an important role if your beneficiaries will need funds after your death to help replace your income, pay off debt or provide for college or other expenses. Cash value life insurance has the added feature of allowing net premiums to accumulate in your policy. The life insurance company guarantees that it will pay a minimum interest rate on the cash value.

Advanced life insurance planning can be used to help your loved ones pay a tax bill and retain more of the money you leave to them through other investments, as well.

Life insurance companies sell more than life insurance, though. One other insurance product, which we discussed in Chapter 2, is an annuity. Remember, an annuity is a contract you enter into with an insurance company in which the company promises to take the money you put into a contract, the principal, and return it to you in systematic guaranteed payouts beginning either immediately or at a point of your choosing in the future.

The guarantees provided by an annuity are backed by the financial strength and claims-paying ability of the insurance company issuing the contract. The annuity value can grow via the various ways the insurance company might credit interest to your contract. But, an annuity is usually very limited in terms of liquidity. It is not a product from which you should expect to get your money back immediately should you encounter an emergency need for cash.

You may remember, a fixed or fixed index annuity credits interest based on either a minimum guaranteed rate of interest or the performance of an external market index such as the S&P 500©, respectively. A fixed index annuity limits the amount of interest each year—in the form of a cap, spread or a participation rate—meaning the interest credited to your account value might not be as great as the rise in the market in any one year. But, this annuity also has a "floor," meaning that in a year with negative market growth, your contract value may not be credited anything, but neither will it lose money because of that negative market activity.

Annuities, in short, can work to provide a consistent income stream, not unlike a pension, which can be important in a time when defined benefit pensions are a dying breed.

Some of the annuities will guarantee an income for life, based on the strength of the issuing insurance company. There are a lot of insurance companies we really like to work with, and we do our due diligence on our end. Ideally, you would work with an insurance company that has very strong ratings and very strong financials and with a financial professional who's going to make sure they only recommend those companies.

How do we make sure we are choosing the right options? Well here are some guidelines to follow, generally. First, rate the attributes you seek in an investment in order of importance.

- Do you need income first and desire guarantees?
- Do you want growth first and desire income second?
- What is most important to you about this investment?
- Do you need protection and liquidity?
- Are you willing to assume some risk for a potentially higher return?

Figuring out the attribute that is most important to you and selecting the second-most-important attribute can help point you in the right direction faster.

It's important to find a financial professional who can help you access any number of different financial products. Be sure you understand if the financial professional you work with receives incentives to sell you certain types of products or services. At Kelly Capital Partners, we incorporate both the insurance and the investment world; we don't have a bias with either one and each plays a powerful role when combined.

Consider it this way: Would you hire a home remodeling contractor who carried only a hammer on his tool belt? Is this a person best equipped to deal with the myriad of issues that inevitably pop up on a home improvement project? There is an expression that says when you only have a hammer, every problem looks like a nail. In the context of our discussion here about retirement planning, this means you likely won't realize all your retirement goals if you don't have the full inventory of financial tools available.

Finally, we suggest you seek out "true diversification" within your portfolio first. Then, seek diversification among asset allocation and asset classes second. Instead, you might separate your assets by your objectives. One category might be financial products that handle your protection and income needs, another might be investments that handle growth and wealth management needs, and another asset class like bank accounts that give you the liquidity or emergency access you need.

A quick Google search or browse through top headlines in financial magazines shows there is little industry consensus as to what constitutes the field of retirement income planning.

While professionals generally agree they must help clients replace sources of income and that expenses are unknown and uncertain, the way companies or individuals go about helping their clients can be greatly hindered by biases in backgrounds (going back to that investment vs. insurance mindset we touched on earlier). There are not necessarily any inherently bad financial products, but any product could be sold inappropriately, sold to someone for whom it doesn't work within the broader context of their retirement income plan for their goals and needs. When these products are used correctly, then they can work very well. The negativity surrounding annuities is a perfect example. There are situations where a consumer was sold an annuity that didn't fit their needs, just as there are times that perhaps someone could have benefitted from having an annuity as part of their plan but it was not included.

The financial services industry is presented with a tremendous marketplace opportunity with the baby boomers retiring, and with that has come competition. It's good for the consumer that the industry has been innovative in developing new products to match the ever-changing needs of retirees today. But everyone knows there's only one kind of money. It's green and it's the kind you spend, right? Not exactly.

In a properly structured plan, we use a combination of short-term and long-term vehicles to help provide clients with a balance of protection, liquidity and growth, all bent toward income. At every stage of your life, you face important decisions with your retirement savings. Deciding upon which vehicles you choose for your money may impact your finances for the rest of your life and the legacy you might leave behind.

Different Times of Life, Different Goal, Different Investments

The common goal of any investment is to make money. That much is obvious. What is less obvious, however, is how we accomplish that goal at different stages of our lives when different aspects of risk, protection, growth and liquidity all must be considered in the investments we make.

Let's consider two different examples at opposite ends of the investment life cycle. The first is a 22-year-old woman, just starting her career after finishing college. She is smart enough to know she wants to invest in her future, but her immediate limitations are an entry-level wage, dealing with regular monthly expenses that come from living on her own (perhaps for the first time), and possibly the prospect of student loans. Despite all the demands on her limited income, she still takes the advice of parents or mentors and finds a way to "pay herself first," which in her case means setting aside $100 a month for investment. Good for her.

Our example at the other end of the investment spectrum is a 60-year-old woman approaching the end of an established career. She's likely been investing in some way—perhaps in an employer-sponsored retirement plan like a 401(k) or an individual IRA—throughout her working career. But now she has reached a point where she has just finished paying off a child's college debts and she finds she can invest another $2,000 monthly.

Question: Should an advisor steer these same two women into the same kind of portfolio? Answer: Of course not.

These two different women at different parts of their lives have vastly different needs even as they have a common goal of making money on their investments.

The younger woman is seeking long-term growth and is likely more willing to accept a higher level of risk in the hope of receiving a greater long-term reward. She is young enough that she has time to invest for the long-term. Investors who start early, while there are years of earnings ahead, can afford to build a more aggressive portfolio with hopes of higher potential gains. Although the stock market will be up and down in the short-term, historically it has been a good wealth-building tool over the long term.

Her older counterpart, on the other hand, can't afford to be as adventurous with money she will be needing relatively soon, as income in retirement.

Her tolerance for risk is most likely relatively low, but she also understands the pitfalls of being overly conservative. Putting that money in a perfectly safe bank account paying 0.05 percent interest—a typical rate for many accounts in 2018—will likely mean she will lose money to inflation over the long term. So, it may be appropriate for her to invest in lower-risk, lower-reward investment options—perhaps in government bonds—that may be too conservative an investment for her much younger friend, but may stay just ahead of the inflation rate and provide a relatively stable return.

The point that bears repeating here is that retirement is just another phase, as opposed to representing the end, of our investment lives. Investing approaches that worked well for us during the accumulation phase of our lives now should be adjusted as we enter the distribution stage. Thoughts of income, protection and liquidity might now take precedence over growth, although some portion of a portfolio may still need to target growth that at least keeps up with inflation. Finding a financial professional to help you make those adjustments and find the proper mix of investments can be a critical part of the overall success of your retirement plan.

CHAPTER 9

Withdrawal Strategies

"Money never made a man happy yet, nor will it.
There is nothing in its nature to produce happiness.
The more a man has, the more he wants.
Instead of filling a vacuum, it makes one."
~ Ben Franklin

I t's essential for retirees to have a plan for withdrawing money from their various accounts and contracts. It needs to be a plan that meets their changing needs and expenses throughout their post-working years. Numerous factors go into developing this withdrawal strategy. For instance, are you more concerned with tax efficiency or longevity risk?

There are three tax categories of vehicles from which you can draw income in retirement.

The first is pre-tax or tax-deferred accounts, which includes individual retirement accounts (IRAs) as well as 401(k)s, 403(b)s and the like. The money you contributed to these accounts is not subject to income tax at the time of the contribution but ordinary income tax will be due when you take the money out of the account.

Roth IRAs and Roth 401(k) accounts make up the second category. These are retirement accounts to which you contribute funds upon which you've already paid ordinary income tax. Roth IRAs accumulate value without tax on their earnings and allow you to take distributions from the accounts tax-free, as long as you are following their well-defined tax rules. Among Roth requirements for taking advantage of tax-free distributions: you must be age 59 ½ to take distributions from the account without incurring a penalty, and you must wait five years after your first initial Roth contribution before you can take a distribution. You aren't required to take RMDs from a Roth IRA, but keep in mind you do need to take RMDs from Roth 401(k) accounts.

The third category is taxable investment accounts, such as brokerage accounts and mutual funds. Unlike distributions taken from pre-tax accounts such as the traditional IRA or 401(k) in which you pay income tax on both the principal invested and any investment gain, distributions from taxable accounts—those funded with post-tax dollars—include taxes only on any profit (also known as capital gains) realized from the sale of the assets. These capital gains taxes come at a lower rate than ordinary income taxes; currently the three long-term capital gains brackets are at 0 percent, 15 percent and 20 percent.

It's important to decide which account or assets you will liquidate first to meet any cash needs. Should you tap into your Roth account first because those assets are generally distributed tax-free? Or, should you use those assets last, or maybe even leave them to your heirs since they could conceivably grow tax-free for many years?

There is no one right answer. You really need to be careful about which accounts you're taking the money from when you begin taking distributions for income purposes in retirement. If you withdraw funds from one or two of your investment accounts and not from anything else, you could affect your asset allocations strategy, a strategy which helps you ensure diversification and coordinate your accounts so they work together.

What sometimes makes sense from a tax standpoint can occasionally make things worse for your risk tolerance, another one of several things to keep in mind when deciding from which accounts you will take distributions. Let's say, for instance, you had what you considered a proper risk/reward balance of stocks and bonds, a mix you considered suitable for your current age. But after taking distributions and income from, say, your bond accounts, you suddenly find yourself top-heavy in the more aggressive stock or speculative assets you maintained in the hope of generating some inflation-beating growth. Your balance has now been thrown off. Affecting risk tolerance is something you should consider when taking withdrawals, just as you should consider keeping withdrawals at a level that doesn't elevate you into a higher tax bracket.

Inflation also is going to continue to have a similar effect and can cause a dramatic decrease in the buying power of our dollars. Historically, the stock market has outpaced inflation over the long term, although there's no way to predict that this will continue to happen. Cash can lose its value due to inflation in the low-interest climate of today. While investing conservatively might feel safe in the short-term, you're potentially exposing your dollars to a loss of purchasing power due to the lower returns you are likely to receive with these conservative investments. It's important to make sure you have a strong balance between protection and growth.

From a tax perspective, it is important to consider how your assets may be allocated in the three broad tax categories we discussed earlier in this chapter and how the different tax characteristics of these accounts may be appropriate for you. Accounts that are taxed differently when you withdraw from them can be important later on depending on your circumstances at the time.

We talked about this in another chapter, but it bears repeating here. You also might want to consider converting some of your pre-tax money from a traditional IRA into Roth accounts, either a Roth IRA or a Roth 401(k) (if you had previously established this kind of employer-sponsored retirement plan).

Keep in mind the rules here. The money you convert from a traditional IRA into a Roth IRA becomes taxable as ordinary income in the year you make the conversion. But, remember also that earnings in the Roth will continue to grow tax-free, and you will not pay tax upon taking a qualified distribution. Moreover, Roth IRA accounts are not subject to RMDs during the owner's life (though Roth 401(k) plans are), and, as long as you follow the rules, Roth plans can be passed on to heirs without your loved ones paying the taxes that come with inherited IRAs.

There are optimal times to convert to Roths. We find you're more likely to want to do it when you're going to be in a lower income tax bracket and consequently pay less in taxes on the money you convert. That time could be right after you retire, or before you start to take Social Security. Or, if you're going to be switching jobs and might not be working for a short period of time, you could find yourself in a lower tax bracket for that particular year, giving you an opportunity to realize a lower tax rate when doing a Roth conversion.

A common strategy is to stretch out Roth IRA conversions over a period of several years, often early in retirement when your income is reduced and you might find yourself in a lower tax bracket. The idea here is not to do too big a Roth conversion at any one time as the tax hit can be considerable if you do too much in any one year.

Also keep in mind when taking withdrawals that assets with fluctuating values are generally not considered appropriate for basic needs or emergency funds. If the market takes a downturn in your retirement years, you should have a source of funds from which to take income without having to sell assets when market values are depressed. The key here is to maintain a balance between conservative money—such as money in assets that are not subject to market fluctuations—and enough in growth-focused assets to hopefully replace at least part of what you withdraw for income.

To illustrate the importance of the income/growth balance, consider the plight of some people who retired around the time of the Great Recession in 2008 and immediately found themselves in a difficult situation. When the stock market crashed, retirement accounts lost about 30 percent of their value. That caused retirees to rethink their withdrawal strategies and really question the 4 percent withdrawal rule.[25]

The 4 Percent Rule and Other Conventional Wisdom

Many retirees have at least a basic understanding of the "4 percent rule," one of the more easily understood concepts about how to turn retirement savings into retirement income.

This rule holds, in effect, that a typical retiree can withdraw up to 4 percent from his retirement nest egg each year and have an 80 to 90 percent chance of seeing that nest egg survive for 30 years, even after adjusting for inflation. This concept was developed around 1994 after William Bengen, a financial planner, tested multiple withdrawal rates against historical market rates of return—i.e., money coming in to partially supplement money going out—to find a withdrawal rate that could stand the test of time.

In a common application of the 4 percent rule, a retiree with $500,000 in retirement savings could withdraw $20,000 a year (4 percent) from those accounts as a supplement for Social Security, pension or work income he might also receive. The strategy calls for an annual adjustment for inflation, meaning in year two, our sample retiree might withdraw an additional 2 percent, or $20,400. The next year he adds another 2 percent (or whatever figure reflects the inflation rate that year) to

---

[25] AARP Public Policy Institute. December 2008. "The Impact of the Financial Crisis on Older Americans."
https://assets.aarp.org/rgcenter/econ/i19_crisis.pdf.

that total. In Bengen's theory, a retirement nest egg will survive without running out of money amid different market performances—where in theory there will be more up years than down years—for at least 30 years.[26]

Well, like any theory, the 4 percent rule is anything but a set-in-stone fact of life, even if it has become something of a "conventional wisdom" piece in the financial advice community. To its credit, the 4 percent rule is simple to understand, and many people unfamiliar with the myriad aspects of financial planning tend to gravitate to things that are easy to understand.

But life is anything but simple or predictable. I am the youngest of five children in my family, and I'm the fourth girl, much to my only brother Larry's dismay. When my parents brought me home, my father proudly walking up the sidewalk, happy to have another healthy child to add to his household, Larry—at age 4—strode boldly up to our father and kicked him—BAM!—right in the shin. As my parents stared at this brassy, angry child, he glared back, "You said it was going to be a boy!" I can imagine our three sisters, Cyndi, Maureen and Jo-Ann, must have given him a just cause for that outburst. Cute, but I think it makes my point: Nothing is certain.

None of us know how long we will live, or what our health will be like in the time we have left. Nor can anyone accurately predict the ups and downs of the market, trends sometimes controlled by non-economic world

---

[26] Randall Smith. Investopedia. "Why the 4% Retirement Rule Is No Longer Safe."
https://www.investopedia.com/articles/personal-finance/120513/why-4-retirement-rule-no-longer-safe.asp.

events that can't be foreseen. There are, of course, reasonable precautions we can take in retirement planning. We can, for example, maintain an age-reasonable mix of stocks and bonds with a realistic expectation of positive long-term returns. We can talk about strategic income withdrawal and tax planning. But the bottom line that must be understood is that forces outside our control can sometimes wreak havoc on even the best of retirement plans.

This is why your retirement plan should have distribution options that involve more than the "conventional wisdom" of the 4 percent plan. For, even if you accept a 4 percent annual distribution as a supplemental income target, you still must be smart in the selection of your various retirement accounts from which you will get that income. It's here that you need to develop an individual withdrawal strategy—one that is unique to you—to help you reach whatever income goal you might set for yourself.

Tapping Taxable vs. Tax-Deferred Accounts

While you certainly want a withdrawal plan that works best for your individual situation, there are some general rules of thumb that can be helpful in developing a plan.

One such general rule holds that it is usually more advantageous to take income by selling assets held in taxable accounts—assets you purchased with after-tax money—than it is to take your first distributions from tax-deferred accounts such as an IRA or 401(k).

The reasoning goes that distributions taken from tax-deferred accounts are taxed as ordinary income, a rate higher than that imposed on capital gains. You may re-call that we talked earlier about how you pay only a cap-ital gains tax—or possibly can write off a capital gains loss—when selling assets from taxable accounts, those upon which you already have been taxed. Assets in tax-deferred accounts, on the other hand, have never been taxed, which means Uncle Sam expects you to pay a higher ordinary income tax on any income produced by the sale of such assets.

Another advantage to keeping money in qualified (tax-deferred) accounts for as long as possible is the chance to continue tax-deferred compound growth. That growth will continue until you are obligated to begin taking fully taxable required minimum distribu-tions (RMDs) starting at age 70 ½.

Keep in mind, too, that the overall tax effect of distri-butions should be a consideration when developing your withdrawal strategy. We will say this again because it is an important point: When it comes to saving for retire-ment, what matters most is not how much you earned and saved throughout your working years, but how much you keep. In short, what you retain in after-tax wealth is the most important figure here.

Proactive Tax Planning

Proactive tax planning is a critical piece of your retire-ment planning. I can't stress enough how important tax planning in retirement is. During your working years, you put money away in employer-sponsored accounts, investing accounts, educational accounts, etc., and, as your income rises, your income is taxable at higher and higher rates. At retirement, you get to choose what type of account you take income from. Money you pull out of IRAs are taxed dollar for dollar, qualified distributions from Roth IRAs isn't taxed at all, your cost basis on money in your checking is not taxed.

Based on my observations, most people exercise what I call reactive tax planning, which means the year has already happened, and you hand your CPA all of your statements and you pray. We promote proactive tax planning; we partner with your tax advisor or accountant to understand your tax situation, and before the year starts we know exactly how much income you're looking for and we help you create a strategy to withdraw income from various account types that can help minimize taxes.

How much and from what accounts you take your income in retirement should be well thought out because one thing affects another. Withdrawing tax-deferred money could affect the taxability of your Social Security benefits, which could in turn push you into a higher income tax bracket. ... There's a domino effect here you want to avoid.

So, the goal for you is very simple before any other planning happens. The goal for you is to know how much money you are looking for every month in income at retirement. Once you have your target for net after-tax income, then we will assist you in determining a withdrawal strategy that tries to minimize taxes. Because if you don't have to pull as much out from your accounts because you're not paying as much in taxes, the longer your money stays in your investments, still earning potential returns and compounding year after year.

The Effect of RMDs

Let's take a minute here to take a closer look at the effects RMDs can have on your all-important after-tax wealth. In doing so, we will begin to uncover what we believe is a flaw in the rule of thumb described before that would have us take income almost exclusively from taxable accounts first while delaying the harvesting of tax-deferred accounts until later.

The drawback, as noted earlier, is those tax-deferred accounts must be tapped eventually; the IRS requires you to do so. And unless you do something to draw down the level of those tax-deferred accounts prior to the start of RMDs, the tax bite incurred on large required distributions can be both unexpected and significant. Bottom line, these required distributions—money you may not want or need to take but must take anyway—could very well elevate you into a higher tax bracket, the result of which is reduced tax efficiency and after-tax wealth.

A 2011 study prepared by Lewis Coopersmith, an associate professor of management sciences at Rider University, and Alan Sumutka, a CPA and associate professor of accounting at Rider, suggests a retiree might over the course of his entire retirement actually see greater after-tax wealth by taking first distributions from tax-deferred accounts instead of taxable ones—an opposite approach to conventional wisdom.[27]

---

[27] Lewis W. Coopersmith and Alan R. Sumutka. Journal of Financial Planning. 2011. "Tax-Efficient Retirement Withdrawal Planning Using a Linear Programming Model."

The Coopersmith-Sumutka study essentially looked at the two different withdrawal strategies under a variety of different scenarios. They incorporated factors such as different rates of return on taxable assets versus tax-deferred assets. They compared tax returns using itemized deductions against those with standard deductions.

Without getting too deep into the thick weeds of their study, the authors determined a tax-efficient withdrawal plan that takes early distributions from tax-deferred accounts can, under certain conditions, outperform the conventional wisdom plan of tapping taxable accounts first. Coopersmith and Sumutka, in fact, demonstrated scenarios in which their withdrawal strategy could outperform the conventional wisdom approach by as much as 16 percent.

Now, few people reading this book are likely to be CPAs or associate professors of accounting. No one is asking you to fully understand the detailed metrics of the Coopersmith-Sumutka study. And it's worth noting, 2011 was a few years ago and the tax brackets have shifted somewhat.

Yet, the point to be taken here is there is no one easily defined strategy that spells out the best way to take retirement income. Because your retirement income plan needs to be specific to you, there can't really be a one-size-fits-all approach.

The other point to be made here is, when you seek the help of a retirement professional, make sure you are

---

https://www.onefpa.org/journal/Pages/Tax-Efficient%20Retirement%20Withdrawal%20Planning%20Using%20a%20Linear%20Programming%20Model.aspx.

dealing with someone who understands more than "conventional wisdom." Such an approach might work perfectly well for you, and in many cases it will. Still, if you have some special circumstances—such as those identified in the Coopersmith-Sumutka study—you need a financial professional who is at least aware of different approaches and thinking. You need someone willing to crunch your personal numbers during a yearly review to help you determine a withdrawal strategy aimed at producing the greatest after-tax wealth over a long period of time.

Be sure you are dealing with a professional who takes a long-term view of your retirement. For example: Make sure he or she discusses options to drain down any sizable IRA account you may have, lest that IRA present a major tax event.

Make sure your advisor understands and explains to you the estate planning implications of taxable vs. tax-deferred accounts. People concerned about passing on wealth (of whatever level) to beneficiaries should understand the different tax implications of passing on tax-deferred money (such as that in an IRA) as compared to handing down tax-free money such as that in a Roth account. Drawing down your IRA in your lifetime is viewed by some as a final gift to be given to one's children.

Charlie's Graduation from West Point, 2014.

CHAPTER 10

Looking for a Financial Professional

It's not about the product, it's about the plan.

In our practice, it is about the client, and we simply ask people, "What are your concerns?" Then we help them decide if they are prepared to act to address those concerns. Can their concerns be fixed? If so, we begin the process.

Being financially successful takes knowing your destination and understanding why it is important for you to get there. Not just the logical reasons or benefits, but the emotional reasons. Emotions often dictate our human behavior. A concern is emotional. A financial concern is emotional. A fear is emotional. The first item on your retirement plan should be your biggest concern. When you have identified where you are going, a good financial professional can help you get there. Once you have expressed a goal, it is time to figure out how you can get there. Most financial goals take money.

To reach these goals, we sometimes have to make changes. Many of the changes we help our clients make involve changing investment strategies.

As a financial firm, we can help only if people want us to help, but it's very important that they choose their goals and tell us what their financial concerns are.

The job of a financial firm is to help you reach more financial success than what you could obtain by going it alone, to coach you into establishing realistic goals, and to help you when the going gets tough. Sometimes it means going in a direction that is counter-intuitive, such as delaying saving for retirement in order to pay down debt.

Another counter-intuitive recommendation we sometimes offer is the following: If you must choose between saving for your retirement and saving for your kids' education, then save for retirement. Look at it this way: Your kids can take out student loans or work while in college, or both. Believe me, they will be okay, and maybe even better off because of it. However, if you don't save for your retirement, you could end up living with your well-educated kids.

Tough choices have to be made. That is why it is so important to feel the benefits of the goal. Only then will you be able to make those tough choices and stick with them. Remember to begin with the end in mind: literally write it down. Be crystal clear. We like to begin with our clients writing down what their goals are, then our mission is to help them reach their goal. Get a coach, a financial professional who can help you reach your goal.

One last item to keep in mind: Just as successful athletes focus on one game or match at a time, successful investors focus on one issue at a time. They fix a problem when it arises, and then they move on to the next one.

If a person has a retirement savings plan at all today, it is likely to be in a 401(k), or a similar account. Many Americans approaching retirement do not have sufficient amounts of money saved. Of the money they have saved, much of it is in stocks, mutual funds or other investments subject to the inevitable ups and downs of the market.

Our goal is to help as many people as possible enjoy a greater retirement. We have insurance products that offer substantial guaranteed income benefits no matter what the stock market does. No matter what financial challenges your employer faces, no matter what your pension or 401(k) does, there are insurance products available that can guarantee you income payments for as long as you live. Our job is to help educate you about what such products can offer.

When it comes to retirement planning, asking questions helps organize the process you should go through to make good decisions, so don't be afraid to ask yourself or your financial professional questions such as:

- Do you think taxes will be higher in the future?
- Do you think inflation will increase?

It's all about having the quality of lifestyle we desire. The question we all must address is, what does retirement look like for us? Do we want to feel reasonably assured that we can protect and preserve the quality of our lifestyle, or do we want to be on a roller coaster ride as we travel through our life stages due to unplanned life events, market volatility, taxes we can't control or a host of other unknowns?

This is why it is a good idea to have a solid lifetime income plan in place before you begin thinking about retirement. Life-changing events occur spontaneously. You could find yourself widowed at age 52. Or, the job you think is reasonably secure today might well be gone a year from now. This is why we have to prepare in advance for unexpected contingencies.

How do you create a lifetime income plan that protects your lifestyle?

Decisions determine our destiny, how many of us have heard this but never stopped to ponder what decisions will truly determine our destiny?

The decisions you make throughout your lifetime can have a substantial impact on your financial security, including your retirement. These include decisions like:

- Choosing a career
- Getting married
- Buying a home
- Having children

Why is it we spend more time planning a dinner party, a golf game or vacation than we spend planning for the various stages of our life to help ensure we have economic security? Another alarming point is that we often confuse investing with having a financial strategy. This is a misconception; investing can be part of a plan, but it is not a PLAN.

This is why I can't stress enough, especially as we approach the end of this book, the need for careful, advance planning over a period of years leading up to retirement. We are actually talking about looking at a bigger picture here, one that takes a realistic look at where you are today; where you would like to be in retirement; what have you saved now and what you need to do in the future to achieve the kind of retirement goals you have for yourself. The dream is something you have to make for yourself. Showing you strategies that can help get you there is the job of your financial professional.

The Role of the Fiduciary

Perhaps you've heard some discussion in recent years about the role of the fiduciary in financial planning. If you haven't, don't worry, we'll talk about it here.

The "fiduciary standard," by definition, requires a financial advisor to put the best interest of his or her client above all other considerations, especially his or her own profit, when offering financial recommendations. The fiduciary standard is more demanding than the "suitability standard" that only requires a financial services broker to sell products that are "suitable" to the client purchasing them. What does this mean to the average person planning for retirement?

Well, you truly deserve to know whether the person with whom you are working is giving you financial advice based on your best interests, or whether the investment products being offered are merely suitable for you. Not that there is anything necessarily wrong with a "suitable" investment, but the truth is some financial products are sold based on increased incentives—usually in the form of greater commissions—for the broker making the sale.

The issue is significant enough that the Obama administration in 2015 ordered the Department of Labor to implement a rule change that directed all financial professionals dealing with qualified retirement plans to meet a fiduciary standard by the year 2017. Unfortunately, after significant pushback from members of the financial services industry, the rule's implementation has continued to be delayed—at this point it is unclear when the "DOL Fiduciary Rule" might come into play.

On a personal note, we believe in the fiduciary standard here at Kelly Capital Partners. We have several fiduciaries on staff, which means the retirement advice from those individuals must take the best interests of our client as our first consideration. We firmly believe this is a point you should strongly consider when deciding on the professional with whom you will build a customized plan to address your individual retirement goals.

We are independent, so we are not tied to any bank or any brokerage firm or any insurance company. We don't have to be a champion of any particular product, strategy or company, we are free to do whatever is in the client's interests. We are the ones meeting with the clients, day-in and day-out, so we are the ones making the decisions. There's no one in New York telling us what to do with your money. We are the ones hearing about your goals, hearing about your dreams and your future and helping you get there, so we're the ones collaborating with you in your decision making.

Let's take a minute here and talk about what it means to you when you deal with a completely independent agent, as opposed to one tied to, say, a large national company.

The difference, in short, can be in the vast variety of financial options available to you through an independent agent who has access to a multitude of companies. This is often in contrast to the broker working for a big-name financial services company whose firm is receiving incentives to promote, for example, the products of a particular mutual fund company. This is not an illegal practice, mind you. The products being promoted may be perfectly suitable for your purposes, but the bottom line remains that a client sometimes isn't getting a full array of options.

It's important for you, the consumer, to know about this, because you are not working in the financial services industry every day like we are, so you may not be aware when this goes on, but we think it's important to remind you that it's something to keep in mind.

You might be asking yourself—how do I know if my advisor is of the fiduciary standard or if my advisor is of the suitability standard? One easy telltale way is to know if you are with an advisor or broker who specializes in one product, or maybe just a few products, then it's possible you're not working with a fiduciary. Brokers and advisors who specialize in only a few types of financial products are sometimes biased. Either the firm makes them operate this way or they themselves choose to work this way. A fiduciary advisor will often spend more time on the logistics of your situation and the ins and outs of your needs and less time on selling you specific products or pitching you investments. This is mainly because they can offer almost any financial product they are appointed to sell.

I met a couple who had about $700,000 of total investments. They had sought the advice of an advisor who had recommended that he put all of that money, except for $20,000, into an annuity, so the plan was for all the money to go into one annuity for income payouts, but that only left $20,000 liquid for the rest of his life. This was a 63-year-old and his wife. They had a lot of years to live being tied down to this annuity and the income that would come out of it. Moreover, he was the annuity's sole beneficiary, also known as the "single payout," so this did not even plan for his wife. If this man had died young for some reason or predeceased his wife, under the contract terms, she would not have even received the income available. Luckily, he had not signed the paperwork yet, so he had time to find a better solution to balancing his need for protection, growth and liquidity.

It just really comes down to making sure your financial professional is not biased, and definitely always, always get a second opinion. I mean, you get a second opinion for your health. You go to two or three doctors to make sure you are getting the best medical advice. I strongly suggest you do the same thing with your financial approach. This is your life. This is your retirement life. You've got to make sure you take care of it.

Annual brothers trip, London 2017.

About the Author

Janie Kelly, RICP®, is Managing Partner of Kelly Capital Partners. She serves clients through her team, coordinating the numerous components of an individual's financial and retirement income approach and by providing insurance strategies and proactive personal service. Her focus is on helping retirees attain confidence in their financial future through a well-designed strategy they can rely on throughout their retirement years.

The team's comprehensive planning consists of income planning, investment planning, tax planning strategies, legacy planning concepts, and health care planning. Janie has her Retirement Income Certified Professional (RICP®) designation, along with her Michigan life and health insurance license. She is a graduate of Michigan State University.

Janie and her husband, Pat, are the proud parents of four boys. Three of their sons are Michigan State graduates, one is a West Point USMA graduate.

Contact Us

For more information on how to create a comprehensive retirement income strategy for your personal finances, please feel free to reach out to our firm or tune into "Kelly Capital Retirement Talk" on Saturdays at 9 a.m. on WMUZ 103.5 FM in the Southfield area.

Kelly Capital Partners
29100 Northwestern Highway, Suite 320
Southfield, MI 48034
248.262.7217 | info@kellycapitalpartners.com

Made in the USA
Monee, IL
26 August 2019